Cheshire Railways

IN OLD PHOTOGRAPHS

To Bethan

Cheshire Railways

IN OLD PHOTOGRAPHS

MIKE HITCHES

Alan Sutton Publishing Limited
Phoenix Mill · Far Thrupp · Stroud
Gloucestershire

First Published 1994

Copyright © Mike Hitches

British Library Cataloguing in Publication Data.
A catalogue record for this book is available from
the British Library.

ISBN 0-7509-0756-8

Typeset in 9/10 Sabon.
Typesetting and origination by
Alan Sutton Publishing Limited.
Printed in Great Britain by
Hartnolls, Bodmin, Cornwall.

Contents

Introduction

Covering an area of north-west England stretching from the north Wales border to the outskirts of Manchester, and including the Wirral peninsula, which lies between the Dee and Mersey estuaries, and the outer edge of Liverpool, Cheshire's railway history dates back to that form of transport's earliest days. The county's first trunk line was the Grand Junction Railway, opened in July 1837. The GJR formed part of a link between London and the important north-western cities of Liverpool and Manchester. The connection was completed by the famous, and very profitable, Liverpool and Manchester Railway, opened in 1830 as the first true 'inter-city' passenger railway, and the London and Birmingham Railway, opened to through traffic in 1838. The GJR ran from Birmingham to Earlestown, and cut through the heart of Cheshire. Once the GJR proved profitable, other lines were opened to take advantage of traffic from the county's salt-production industry. These lines eventually linked the Merseyside docks and Manchester with Chester, Crewe and destinations further south, as well as linking London with Dublin via the Chester and Holyhead Railway. The rail network in the county was, more or less, fully established before the second half of the nineteenth century.

Until the 1923 Grouping, several companies operated services into Cheshire, including the North Staffordshire Railway, the Great Western Railway and the Cheshire Lines Committee (made up of the Great Central Railway, the Great Northern Railway and the Midland Railway), but the most important was the London and North Western Railway. At its formation in 1846 the General Manager was the ex-GJR Secretary, Captain Mark Huish. He had been instrumental in the formation of the new company (which was destined to become the largest joint stock company in the world) following disputes with others over the construction of the Trent Valley Railway, which linked Stafford with Rugby, avoiding congested Birmingham, and he was to assume an important role in the development of Cheshire's railways. After the Grouping, locomotives of the LMS, GWR and LNER were seen at the head of trains operating within the county, a situation that continued until the end of steam on British Railways.

To house the numerous locomotives working through the county, Cheshire was blessed with several large and important locosheds at places such as Crewe, Chester and Birkenhead. The county also had a major locomotive construction and maintenance works at Crewe, whose role was to build and maintain main-line engines for the LNWR and, later, the LMS and BR. Crewe was responsible for building some of Britain's most famous locos, as well as more humble tank and tender engines. Crewe works was an important part of Cheshire's economy, as it provided employment for thousands of people in the area, much of the work being highly skilled. Crewe was very much a 'railway town', the railway company providing a great deal of housing for its workers, as well as churches, parks and other leisure facilities. The town's fortunes reflected those of the railway. Even today, a large part of the population work on the railway, although other industries, e.g. Rolls Royce cars, have been established in the town. No doubt Rolls Royce's motive for coming to Crewe was to take advantage of the existing highly skilled workforce.

The most important stations in the county were at Crewe, Chester and Birkenhead. Crewe station served trains on the West Coast Main Line between Glasgow, Liverpool, Manchester, Birmingham and London Euston, along with services along the north Wales coast to Holyhead. Some of the most famous expresses, including 'The Red Rose' from Liverpool to Euston, and 'The Midday Scot' and 'Royal Scot', passed through the station. The famous 'West Coast Postal' mail train also called at Crewe for exchange of mail. Chester had services to Holyhead, Manchester, Crewe, Birkenhead and Euston. Trains using Chester General station included the 'Irish Mail', running between Euston and Holyhead, and the GWR's Paddington–Birkenhead expresses. Birkenhead Woodside station was the terminus of the GWR expresses from Paddington. These connected with the Woodside Ferry for Liverpool, thereby offering an alternative route to that of the LNWR from Euston to Liverpool Lime Street. The GWR at one time even ran a direct service from Paddington to Liverpool Central, joining the underground system below the Mersey at Rock Ferry.

Much has changed on the railways in Cheshire following the 1960s 'Beeching axe', although the important main lines through Chester and Crewe are largely still intact. One main line has, however, disappeared, that being the old GWR/LMS joint line to Birkenhead Woodside. The line still exists as far as Rock Ferry, but the remainder to Woodside station has gone, as has the station itself. Many of the branches in Cheshire have also gone. Only part of Crewe locomotive works remains, and the Crewe Heritage Centre serves as a reminder of the great railway history of the town. The centre acts as a stabling point for preserved main-line locos which operate special trains along the north Wales coast line from Crewe to Holyhead. These locos give some indication of what the railway was like in its glory days. Also gone are the old locosheds, now no longer required as BR modernizes its engine fleet.

Cheshire was the first county to benefit from electrification of its main line under the 1955 Modernization Plan. The WCML was electrified between Liverpool and Crewe in the early 1960s, a process that continued through to Euston as the decade progressed. Electrification was nothing new, however, as the Wirral Railway was electric-operated from 1902, and the Mersey Railway system between Rock Ferry and Liverpool Central was also electrified in the same period. In recent years this system has been electrified further, first to Hooton and then to Chester, the latter section being completed in 1993.

In preparing this book I have taken pleasure in selecting photographs which recall the great days of steam in Cheshire, when famous trains and locomotives were a constant presence, and the train was the only way to travel. I have also tried to portray the humble branch lines that thrived or otherwise, with little tank engines pottering up and down lines in attractive rural settings, all of which made up the rich tapestry that was the railway system in Cheshire. I hope that the photographs give as much pleasure to you as they have to me.

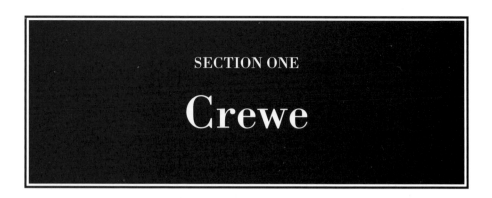

SECTION ONE

Crewe

Until the Grand Junction Railway opened its line between Birmingham and Earlestown, and established a station there, Crewe was no more than a small agricultural village known as Monks Coppenhall. Only a few days before the GJR line was opened, on 4 July 1847, an act authorized construction of the Chester and Crewe and Manchester and Birmingham railways, which started a process that would make Crewe one of the most notable junctions in the world, a status made famous in the days of the music hall. The Crewe–Chester line was opened on 1 October 1840, with the Crewe–Sandbach section of the B&M opening two years later, on 10 August 1842.

As Crewe developed into an important junction, the GJR decided to move its engineering works from Edge Hill, near Liverpool, to the more strategic location, and workshops, along with workers' houses, were constructed around Crewe in preparation for transfer at the beginning of 1843. In March of that year, the embryo Crewe locoworks came into being, turning out its first loco two years later. In 1846 the GJR, along with other companies, became part of the mighty London and North Western Railway, and the new company set about expanding the works, which went on to construct some of the most famous LNWR and LMS locos. The works was responsible for supplying all of the company's engine requirements, from humble tank locos to top-link expresses, and went on to build locos for BR, including steam, diesel and electric types. While much of the old works has been demolished in recent years, Crewe still retains a role in the construction and maintenance of modern locos.

With the establishment of Crewe as a centre for locomotive construction, the town expanded rapidly. It had a population of 30,000 by the turn of the century, and this had doubled by 1950. The railway company provided all community services in the town, including water, gas, hospital, church, law and housing. Crewe works even had its own brickworks to provide building materials, not only for the town but for housing elsewhere on the LNWR system.

As a major railway junction, Crewe was provided with substantial goods facilities to the south of the station, along with large carriage sidings. To provide motive power for the numerous passenger and freight trains in the locality, two large locosheds were built north and south of the station. Crewe North shed, which was situated at the junction of the West Coast Main Line and the line to Chester, housed express engines, while Crewe South shed, close to the marshalling yard, provided goods locos needed in the area.

CREWE LNWR

Platform one at Crewe station in LNWR days, with a north-bound train being loaded with passengers' luggage just prior to departure. A station has existed here since the Grand Junction Railway established its line in 1837. On opening day, in July of that year, a reporter from *The Times* travelled on the first train from Liverpool. His report concerning Crewe read: 'The train reached Crewe at three minutes to 9 o'clock, and was received with a hearty welcome by a large concourse of spectators collected together upon the occasion. There were several parties in carriages from Macclesfield, Congleton, Sandbach, and the neighbourhood. Crewe is 43 miles and a half distant from Liverpool; it is the third station on the line. The train left there at five minutes past 9 o'clock, about half an hour beyond the time fixed. There is a shed built for an extra engine, to assist in propelling the train up the Studeley inclined plain. As yet no engine is assigned to that duty. At half-past 9 o'clock we passed the station house.' Unfortunately, he gives no clue as to what the station building was like, but contemporary drawings show it to be a rather substantial stone structure.

At the northern end of Crewe station is one of the successful LNWR 2–2–2 'Problem' or 'Lady of the Lake' class locos, No. 28, on a local train around 1900, near the end of her life. These Ramsbottom-designed locos were used on top-link expresses in the mid-nineteenth century, often seen at the head of 'The Irish Mail' which ran between Euston and the Irish Sea packet port at Holyhead, on the northern tip of Anglesey in north Wales.

LNWR 'Waterloo' class 2–4–0 No. 742 *Spitfire* at Crewe in 1920, only three years before the Grouping brought the LNWR into the new London, Midland and Scottish Railway.

An ex-LNWR 'Prince of Wales' class 4–6–0 leaves Crewe with an Up express in 1924. The GJR became part of the LNWR in 1846, and under the new company's auspices Crewe station grew apace. When the main line to Stafford was quadrupled in 1876, the station became very congested, and major remodelling was undertaken at Crewe and its approaches by the turn of the century. This remodelling included construction of goods lines under the station to carry freight from Liverpool and Manchester clear of the platforms.

An unnamed ex-LNWR 'Claughton' class 4–6–0 waits at Crewe with a north-bound train in May 1928.

The interior of one of the Travelling Post Offices; most of the LNWR/LMS trains of this type called at Crewe. One such was the famous 'West Coast Postal', which left Euston in the early evening for Glasgow and Aberdeen. The train was featured in the 1935 film *Night Mail*, some of the views being filmed at Crewe, where mail exchange was undertaken and locomotives changed. In those sequences, the train was headed by 'Royal Scot' or 'Patriot' class 4–6–0s, which were virtually new at the time. Other sequences shot at Crewe included views of a new 'Black Five' 4–6–0, an ex-Midland Railway 'Compound' 4–4–0, and a 'Crab' 2–6–0 on the late-arriving Holyhead-bound mail train.

In the final years of the LNWR's existence, a Down express is about to depart from Crewe, with 'Experiment' class 4–6–0 No. 1658 *Flintshire* piloting 'Claughton' class 4–6–0 No. 209 *J. Bruce Ismay*. On the right another LNWR loco is resting from station pilot duties. The ridge-and-furrow station roof and glass screens beyond the platforms are clearly visible.

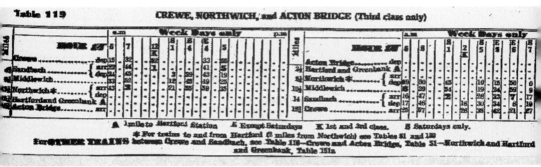

A timetable for the local service between Crewe, Northwich and Acton Bridge in January 1950.

An LNWR postcard portraying its famous 'Scotch Express' approaching Crewe from the south. The train is headed by one of the Francis Webb-designed 4–4–0 express locos. Another LNWR loco can be seen at the entrance to the freight yard, which was, and still is, very substantial, handling great quantities of freight from north-west England and north Wales. On the left of the view is the entrance to Crewe carriage sidings. The picture was taken after the main line to Stafford was quadrupled. Saxby and Farmer-made signals litter the whole layout.

Table 50   LONDON, RUGBY, BIRMINGHAM, WOLVERHAMPTON, STAFFORD, SHREWSBURY, CREWE, MANCHESTER, LIVERPOOL, CHESTER, NORTH WALES, IRELAND, WARRINGTON, PRESTON, CARLISLE, and SCOTLAND

Week Days

Just one page of the substantial timetable for services between Scotland and Euston in January 1950, giving an idea of the number of destinations that could be reached from Crewe in steam days.

The final years of steam traction at Crewe. In this view, on 4 August 1962, the station has already been electrified, but steam is still a common sight. Here, three ex-LMS locos have recently been overhauled at Crewe works, and steamed at Crewe South shed. They are making their way back to Crewe North shed ready for normal duties. In the cavalcade are 'Jubilee' class 4–6–0 No. 45600 *Bermuda*, Fairburn 2–6–4 tank No. 42108, and an unidentified Stanier 'Duchess' Pacific.

BR Standard 'Britannia' class Pacific No. 70047, an unnamed member of the class, bypasses Crewe station as it heads the Up 'Welshman' to Euston on 4 August 1962.

Another 'Britannia' Pacific, No. 70017 *Arrow*, departs from Crewe with a Birmingham to Glasgow express on the same day.

On 4 August 1962, ex-LMS 'Princess-Coronation' Pacific No. 46250 *City of Lichfield* rushes through Crewe station with the Down 'Lakes Express'.

The rather ugly Caprotti valve-geared 'Black Five' 4–6–0 No. 44748 bypasses Crewe station with a train from north Wales to Birmingham in August 1962.

BR Standard class 4 4–6–0 No. 75032 enters Crewe with an empty-stock train on 4 August 1962.

BR Standard class 4 4–6–0, introduced in 1951, waits its turn of duty at Crewe in the late 1950s.

Western Region 0–6–0 pannier tank No. 9630 arrives at Crewe with a local passenger train from Shrewsbury. Although Crewe was very much an LNWR town, other companies were also present there. The North Staffordshire Railway had exchange sidings within sight of the station, and the GWR also had sidings at Gresty Road, along with a small locoshed. Gresty Road sidings could accommodate some 206 wagons and most GWR freight trains received there were sent from Oxley, near Wolverhampton. For many years, difficulties were experienced with engine turning, and considerable time was taken up getting engines to and from Basford Hall. The GWR also had the use of platform bays at the south end of Crewe station for its passenger trains, and the company had its own booking office, passengers' agents office, and lamp and porters' room.

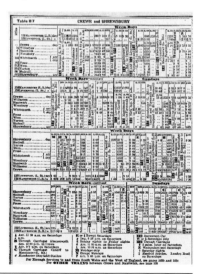

A Western Region timetable for trains operating between Crewe and Shrewsbury.

Ex-LMS Stanier 8F 2–8–0 No. 48424 hauls three 'Jubilee' class 4–6–0s out of Crewe works bound for Crewe South shed on 4 August 1962. The three 'Jubilees' involved in the operation are: 45708 *Resolution*, 45667 *Jellicoe* and 45564 *New South Wales*.

Continuing in the same direction as the previous cavalcade, also on 4 August 1962, is Stanier 8F No. 48424 with the three previously mentioned 'Jubilees'. In the distance, on the right of the picture, is Crewe North Junction signal-box, now incorporated into the Crewe Heritage Centre. The signal-box was opened in 1935, replacing an older LNWR type, and is in the Art Deco style of the period.

A time of transition at Crewe as steam prepares to give way to modern traction. August 1962, and the north end of Crewe station plays host to both the old and the new. The old is in the shape of ex-LMS rebuilt 'Royal Scot' class 4–6–0 No. 46170 *British Legion*, the last of this famous class, while the new are English Electric Type 4 1Co–Co1 diesel-electric loco No. D320 (these were to be best known as Class 40) and 25kv electric BoBo loco No. E3098. The diesel was painted in BR Brunswick green and the electric loco carried a blue livery. The steam loco was also green. Electrification at Crewe was part of a project to bring this new and efficient form of traction to the whole of the West Coast Main Line under the 1955 Modernization Plan. After tests in north-west England, and success in France, of 25kv AC electric overhead systems, BR plumped for this system on the WCML, and in September 1960 the section between Manchester and Crewe was fully electrified. Unfortunately, costs had become prohibitive and work was stopped at Crewe on government orders. After months of pondering at Westminster, Minister of Transport Ernest Marples gave grudging approval for continuation of electrification south of Crewe. It was not until the spring of 1966 that the line from Euston to Liverpool was fully electrified, with the line from Birmingham to Stafford being completed the following year. Once the system was fully operational, advantages in speed and train timings could be fully exploited. By this time, steam had virtually ceased to exist at Crewe.

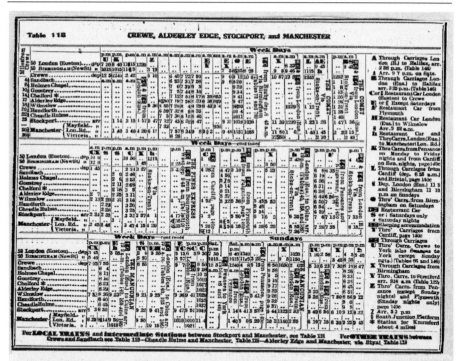

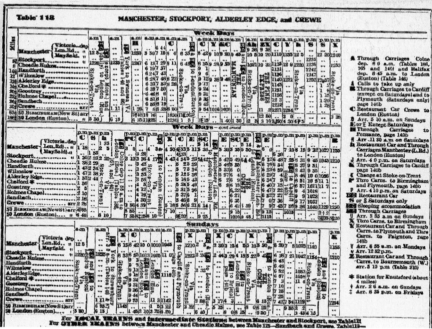

A Crewe–Manchester timetable for January 1950.

An LNWR 'Prince of Wales' class 4–6–0 heads the Up 'Irish Mail' into Crewe from Chester, passing the narrow-gauge railway into Crewe locomotive works, with Crewe North Junction signal-box in the background. A locomotive works was established here by the Grand Junction Railway, which wished to move to this more strategic location from Edge Hill, near Liverpool. The clay soil at Crewe was suitable for the foundations of large buildings and heavy machinery, and the company's wagon works in March 1843, the loco works arriving shortly after. Under LNWR auspices, carriage and wagon construction was moved to Wolverton and Earlestown respectively, but loco construction remained at Crewe. The first loco to be built at Crewe, in 1845, was GJR 2–2–2 *Columbine*, starting a pedigree that was to last for over a century.

The interior of Crewe works at the end of the nineteenth century, with several examples of LNWR engines under construction. In the final years of the nineteenth century the works expanded rapidly, with virtually all of the company's locos being built here, from top-link express engines to freight locos and humble tank engines. In its heyday the works employed thousands in its iron, steel and brass foundries, machine and erecting shops, smithy and boiler shops, as all locos were built, literally, from the ground up, all components being manufactured on site. The majority of those employed in the works were craftsmen, having served long apprenticeships in the type of heavy engineering undertaken at the works. Although Crewe still builds and repairs modern diesel and electric locos, as BREL, nowhere near the number of staff are employed as in steam days, and the vast spaces created by 1980s demolition of the old works have contributed to the high unemployment in Britain today, and the lack of skilled workers. The old railway works here and at places like Swindon and Doncaster provided the necessary skills in the metal trades which once created the nation's wealth in the years prior to the 1980s, when manufacturing became a dirty word.

LNWR 2–4–2 tank No. 1384, one of the many tank engines built at Crewe.

LNWR 'Precedent' class 2–4–0 No. 955 *Charles Dickens*.

'Precursor' class 4–4–0 No. 513, later to become LMS No. 5278. Like that in the previous illustration, it is an example of the express locos built at Crewe for the LNWR.

An ex-LNWR G2 class 0–8–0 freight engine carrying LMS number 9395. Its LNWR number was 485. This was one of the numerous freight engines built at Crewe.

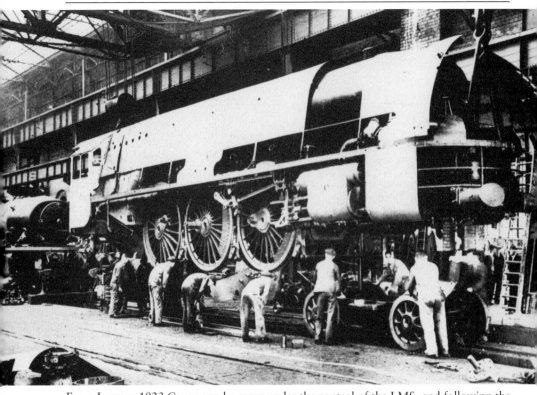

From January 1923 Crewe works came under the control of the LMS, and following the appointment of W.A. Stanier as CME to the LMS in 1931 some of the most famous locos were built there. In 1935 the LNER inaugurated its 'Silver Jubilee' train, running between King's Cross and Edinburgh using the famous streamlined A4 Pacifics, and thereby offering a challenge to the LMS. In response, Stanier designed a streamlined locomotive of his own, the famous 'Princess-Coronation' Pacific. The first of the class, No. 6220 *Coronation*, in blue livery with silver 'speed stripes', was introduced in 1937. On 29 June of that year, the loco attained the speed of 114 mph between Stafford and Crewe, almost coming to grief on the southern approaches to Crewe station. While the train stayed on the rails, all the crockery in the dining car was smashed. The near disaster was caused by the loco having to negotiate a crossover with a 30 mph speed restriction at 58 mph. In this view, one of the streamlined 'Princess-Coronation' locos is under construction at Crewe works. In total thirty-six of these splendid engines were built at Crewe between 1937 and 1939. They were all de-streamlined from 1946.

The predecessors of the 'Princess-Coronation' Pacifics were the twelve 'Princess-Royal' Pacifics, the first LMS Stanier designs of this type. No. 6200 *The Princess Royal* was the first, introduced in 1933; the remainder were built in 1935. One of these, No. 6207 *Princess Arthur of Connaught*, is pictured outside Crewe works in 1935. This loco was the subject of a film made by the LMS about the construction of a loco at the works, and it gave a wonderful insight into the work and craftsmanship involved in the construction of a steam engine.

As well as building locos, Crewe works was also involved in their maintenance and repair. Often certain classes of engine only ever visited Crewe to undergo maintenance work. One such example is illustrated here, an ex-Midland Railway Garratt 2–6–6–2 built by Beyer-Peacock to a Midland design. These locos were usually to be found hauling heavy coal trains out of Toton yards. With so much movement of new and repaired engines, as well as raw materials for the works, an allocation of locos was provided at Crewe works for such duties. In August 1958 the allocation was:

Ex-Midland Railway 3F 0–6–0: 43330 (on loan from Crewe South)
Ex-LMS 4F 0–6–0: 44363, 44373, 44374
Ex-Lancs & Yorks 0–6–0ST: 51412, 51444, 51446
Ex-Lancs & Yorks 3F 0–6–0: 52093, 52201, 52207, 52218, 52225, 52312, 52345, 52441, 52459, 52464
Ex-Caledonian Railway 0–4–0ST: 56027, 56032
Ex-LNWR 2F 0–6–0: 58328, 58347
Total: 21

Most of the locos were of pre-Grouping origin and were almost certainly seeing out their working lives here.

The yard at Crewe North locoshed in March 1964, with BR 'Britannia' Pacific No. 70054 *Dornoch Firth* at the head of a pair of ex-LMS 'Black Five' 4–6–0s. Crewe North was a large locoshed providing motive power for passenger services out of Crewe. Just how important can be judged by its allocation of locos in August 1958:

BR Code 5A
Ex-Midland Railway 2P 4–4–0: 40652, 40655, 40659, 40660, 40679
Ex-LMS Ivatt 2–6–2T: 41220, 41229
Ex-LMS Stanier 2–6–4T: 42575, 42677
Ex-LMS 'Crab' 2–6–0: 42955, 42961, 42963, 42966, 42968
Ex-LMS Stanier 'Black Five' 4–6–0: 44678, 44679, 44680, 44682, 44683, 44684, 44685, 44714, 44758, 44759, 44760, 44761, 44762, 44763, 44764, 44765, 44766, 45021, 45033, 45073, 45113, 45148,45189, 45235, 45240, 45282, 45289, 45369, 45373, 45379, 45390, 45434, 45446
Ex-LMS 'Patriot' class 4–6–0: 45501 *Patriot*, 45503 *The Royal Leicestershire Regiment*, 45507 *The Royal Tank Corps*, 45528, 45529 *Stephenson*, 45544, 45545 *Planet*, 45546 *Fleetwood*, 45548 *Lytham St Annes*
Ex-LMS 'Jubilee' class 4–6–0: 45553 *Canada*, 45556 *Nova Scotia*, 45586 *Mysore*, 45587 *Baroda*, 45591 *Udaipur*, 45604 *Ceylon*, 45617 *Mauritius*, 45623 *Palestine*, 45624 *St Helena*, 45625 *Sarawak*, 45629 *Straits Settlements*, 45630 *Swaziland*, 45634 *Trinidad*, 45643 *Rodney*, 45655 *Keith*, 45666 *Cornwallis*, 45674 *Duncan*, 45678 *De Robeck*, 45684 *Jutland*, 45689 *Ajax*, 45703 *Thunderer*, 45721 *Defiance*, 45726 *Vindictive*, 45733 *Novelty*, 45736 *Phoenix*
Ex-LMS 'Royal Scot' 4–6–0: 46101 *Royal Scots Grey*, 46118 *Royal Welch Fusilier*, 46125 *3rd Carabinier*, 46128 *The Lovat Scouts*, 46129 *The Scottish Horse*, 46134 *The Cheshire Regiment*, 46135 *The East Lancashire Regiment*, 46138 *The London Irish Rifleman*, 46150 *The Life Guardsman*, 46151 *The Royal Horse Guardsman*, 46159 *The Royal Air Force*, 46161 *King's Own*, 46163 *Civil Service Rifleman*
Ex-LMS 'Princess-Royal' 4–6–2: 46203 *Princess Margaret Rose*, 46205 *Princess Victoria*, 46206 *Princess Marie Louise*, 46209 *Princess Beatrice*, 46211 *Queen Maud*, 46212 *Duchess of Kent*
Ex-LMS 'Princess-Coronation' 4–6–2: 46220 *Coronation*, (*continued on page 34*)

(*continued from page 33*) 46221 *Queen Elizabeth*, 46225 *Duchess of Gloucester*, 46228 *Duchess of Rutland*, 46234 *Duchess of Abercorn*, 46235 *City of Birmingham*, 46246 *City of Manchester*, 46248 *City of Leeds*, 46249 *City of Sheffield*, 46251 *City of Nottingham*, 46252 *City of Leicester*, 46253 *City of St Albans*
BR 8P 4–6–2: 71000 *Duke of Gloucester*
Total: 113

Ex-LNWR 'Precursor' class 4–4–0, in LMS guise No. 5279 *Sunbeam* at Crewe, April 1933.

Ex-LNWR 'Prince of Wales' class 4–6–0, as LMS No. 5610 *Robert Southey*, at Crewe in 1930.

Another 'Prince of Wales' class loco at Crewe in 1924. Despite now being under LMS control, the loco still carries its LNWR number 28 on its cast brass plate, and the old company crest remains on the splasher between the first pair of driving wheels.

Ex-LNWR 'Precursor' class 4–4–0 No. 25304 *Greyhound* is piloting rebuilt 'Royal Scot' class 4–6–0 No. 6157 *The Royal Artilleryman* at Crewe a couple of years after the end of the Second World War. The engine by this time was close to the end of its working life.

One of the ubiquitous Stanier 'Black Five' 4–6–0s, No. 44847, at Crewe North shed on 2 August 1963. These locos could be found all over the LMS system and Crewe North was allocated its fair share. In September 1949 it had twenty-eight, rising to thirty-three in August 1958. The shed itself was completely rebuilt in 1959–60, after BR had stated that it was in dire need of substantial repair as early as 1949. The new shed was a concrete and glass structure, and was destined for a short life, closing to steam in June 1965.

BR 'Britannia' Pacific No. 70001 *Lord Hurcomb* in Crewe North shed yard in August 1963. These were the first of the BR Standard locos to be introduced, and all were built at Crewe between the introduction of No. 70000 *Britannia* in 1951, at a cost of £22,573, and the last, No. 70054 *Dornoch Firth*, completed in June 1953 at a cost of £25,331. No. 70001 was, therefore, the second of the class to be completed.

Doyen of the 5XP Stanier 'Jubilee' class 4–6–0s, No. 45552 *Silver Jubilee* at Crewe
North shed in August 1963. Crewe North had a large allocation of these locos for many
years, and No. 45552 was allocated to the shed from June 1961 until September 1964,
when it was withdrawn. The unique feature of this loco was its stainless steel boiler
bands, which are not clearly visible in this photograph.

BR 'Britannia' Pacific No. 70018 *Flying Dutchman* at the entrance to Crewe North shed in August 1963. As modernization of BR motive power began to bite into the express steam fleet, these famous locos lost their role as the main source of power for expresses such as the 'Irish Mail' and 'Royal Scot', these duties going to diesel-electrics from the late 1950s. In order to find useful work for them, as they were only a decade old by this time, most of the 'Britannias' were allocated to Crewe North from 1959 to 1965 and used on expresses and fitted freights along the north Wales coast and the WCML. The same fate befell the Stanier 'Duchess' Pacifics, and they also appeared on the north Wales coast, hauling expresses between Holyhead and Crewe in the first half of the 1960s, until replaced by diesels.

An Ex-LNWR 0–8–4 tank loco at Crewe South shed. No. 7935, ex-LNWR 256, is pictured here in 1935. Crewe South provided locos for huge quantities of freight traffic emanating from the marshalling yard situated here, as the allocation for August 1958 shows:

BR code 5B
Ex-LMS 'Crab' 2–6–0: 42776, 42777, 42785, 42787, 42811, 42813, 42815, 42885, 42894, 42920, 42926, 42933, 42935, 42937, 42939, 42940, 42944
Stanier 'Crab' 2–6–0: 42948, 42950, 42952, 42953, 42956, 42959, 42962, 42964, 42972, 42980, 42983, 42984
Ex-MR 3F 0–6–0: 43187, 43207, 43389, 43410, 43562
Ex-LMS 4F 0–6–0: 44301, 44344, 44359, 44385, 44592, 44595
Ex-LMS 'Black Five' 4–6–0: 44681, 44713, 44834, 44868, 44871, 45000, 45002, 45003, 45044, 45045, 45048, 45060, 45067, 45074, 45108, 45128, 45131, 45149, 45188, 45198, 45270, 45299, 45300, 45301, 45391
Ex-LMS 3F 'Jinty' 0–6–0T: 47280, 47330, 47384, 47414, 47450, 47467, 47516, 47523, 47524, 47526, 47595, 47608, 47670, 47680
Ex-LMS Stanier 8F 2–8–0: 48111, 48174, 48248, 48251, 48255, 48256, 48257, 48262, 48263, 48287, 48289, 48291, 48292, 48294, 48297, 48411, 48516, 48529, 48548, 48626, 48630, 48633, 48659, 48692, 48693, 48734, 48736, 48743, 48764
Ex-LNWR 7F 0–8–0: 48922, 49048, 49158, 49180, 49229, 49407, 49417, 49454
Ex-Lancs & Yorks 0–4–0ST: 51218
Ex-MR 2F 0–6–0: 58135, 58271
Total: 119

Ex-LNWR 'Cauliflower' class 0–6–0 No. 8429 (LNWR No. 319) at Crewe in 1932. In LMS days these locos could be found at Crewe South employed on freight work in the yards.

Ex-LNWR 0–8–2 tank No. 1185, as LMS No. 7870, at Crewe in July 1933.

Another ex-LNWR loco at Crewe in 1936. This is an example of the company's 4–6–2 tanks. Here it carries the LMS number 6993, but it was originally LNWR No. 2292.

Another ex-LNWR 0–8–2 tank, LMS No. 7880, at Crewe in April 1935.

Used as shunting locos in the marshalling yards at Crewe South in LNWR and LMS days, until replaced by 'Jinty' 0–6–0 tanks, were 0–6–0 saddle tanks known as 'Special Tanks' by the old companies. One example, LNWR No. 3315, is seen at Crewe as LMS No. 7370 in 1935.

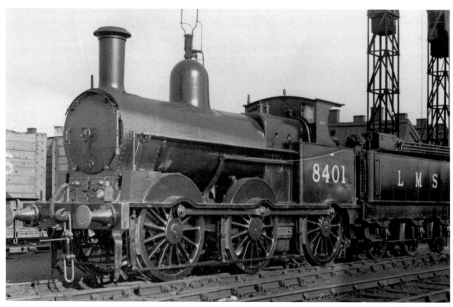

Ex-LNWR 'Cauliflower' class No. 8401 is seen in the yard at Crewe in the 1930s. These engines were nicknamed 'Cauliflowers' because in LNWR days they carried the company's crest on the centre splasher, which looked similar to the vegetable.

An ex-LNWR 0–6–0 coal engine at Crewe in 1935. This loco carries the LMS number 8172, but was originally LNWR No. 3535.

A heavy 0–8–0 freight engine, formerly of the LNWR, LMS G1 class No. 9032 (LNWR No. 1838). This loco was originally a Francis Webb three-cylinder Compound class D, later rebuilt as a simple expansion engine. These locos were very successful, and were widely used on heavy freight work until replaced by Stanier 8F 2–8–0s. They managed to survive, however, well into the BR era, Crewe South shed having eight in 1958, and some lasted until 1963. Crewe South shed closed to steam on 6 November 1967.

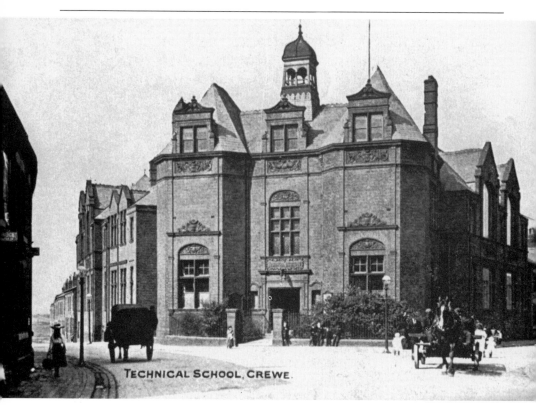

TECHNICAL SCHOOL, CREWE.

Crewe was very much a railway town, the Grand Junction Railway establishing its loco works here in 1843. In preparation, the company built houses ready to transfer its workers from Edge Hill. From that time Crewe expanded rapidly from a small village to a busy town. The LNWR, which took over the GJR in 1846, provided the town with its church, municipal buildings and technical school, which is portrayed here. In the early days the railway company was quite strict with its tenants, encouraging temperance among the workers, and anyone who was found drunk was in danger of losing his home. The LNWR at one time even tried to tell its employees how to vote in one of the general elections, but this not surprisingly led to some trouble for the company.

Victoria Street, Crewe, one of the shopping thoroughfares in the town. This turn-of-the-century view shows the fashions of the day, and a horse-bus completes the scene.

Another view of Victoria Street, Crewe, with a large number of local children posing for the photographer. Most of the boys in this group would eventually find their way into the railway works, or become employees of the LNWR.

Nantwich Road, Crewe, one of the residential streets of the town. Children are playing in the middle of the road, something that would definitely not be possible today. The growth in car ownership did much to damage the railway industry, bringing about a loss of railway employment in the town.

Hightown, Crewe, at the turn of the century. What appears to be a chapel is visible on the left, and housing is on the right. In the background is the church spire, the church being provided by the LNWR. The columns inside the church look to be made of marble, but are in fact cast iron (made in the works) painted to give a marble effect.

SECTION TWO

LNWR Routes

The most important railway company in Cheshire, the LNWR, had several lines radiating from Crewe to Manchester, Liverpool and Chester, all of which still exist today. Its prestige line, however, was the West Coast Main Line between Euston and Glasgow; the section between Warrington (north of Crewe) and Whitmore (south of Crewe) is within Cheshire. All these lines, except that between Chester and Crewe, are now electrified. Part of the old Liverpool and Manchester Railway also passes through the county, near Warrington.

These lines have carried some of the most famous express trains in Britain, and have seen many of the top-link locomotives of both the LNWR and LMS.

An unidentified 'Princess-Coronation' or 'Duchess' Pacific at the head of an express train on the West Coast Main Line south of Crewe.

One of the ubiquitous Stanier 'Black Five' 4–6–0s on a mail train south of Crewe.

Diesel traction tends to be associated with the 1955 Modernization Plan, but the LMS, along with other companies of the 'Big Four', had been experimenting with new types of traction since the end of the Second World War. The LMS had introduced a range of 0–6–0 diesel shunters in the 1930s, but had not been seriously involved in dieselization for use on the main line until the 1940s. Following the war the LMS embarked on an experiment with diesel-electric traction, when the CME at Derby, H.A. Ivatt, worked in conjunction with the English-Electric Company to produce two 1Co–Co1 locomotives, which were to be the forerunners of modern main-line diesels. The first, No. 10000, emerged from Derby works in the first week of December 1947, only a month before nationalization, giving the company time to put its LMS legend on the new engine. The second loco, No. 10001, emerged from Derby early in 1948 as a BR machine. These two locos worked double-headed on the West Coast Main Line, as seen here at the head of a Euston-bound train south of Crewe.

OVER & WHARTON. L.N.W.R.

An LNWR 2–4–2 tank at the head of a single-car railmotor train at the terminus of the branch from the main GJR line, between Earlestown and Crewe, to Winsford. The little branch was opened in 1882 by the LNWR to take advantage of potential salt traffic, a product for which the town was famous. The junction of the branch was a little north of the main-line Winsford station, but its terminus was called Over & Wharton to avoid a name-clash with the station of the Cheshire Lines Committee in the town. The station buildings were simple wooden affairs, as the main reason for building the branch had more to do with freight than passengers. The branch had half a dozen sidings to salt and other works, and a goods yard was provided at the station. The station, along with the branch, was closed to passengers in 1947 and, after a steady decline, to freight traffic in October 1982. The branch served another purpose in the 1960s when, following rapid withdrawal of steam traction, redundant locos were stored there prior to being despatched for scrap.

One of the LMS Fowler 5XP 'Patriot' or 'Baby Scot' 4–6–0s, with the unusual number of 5936, suggesting that it was one of the class that was a rebuild of the famous LNWR 'Claughton' 4–6–0s, on a short oil train at the water troughs near Moore, just south of Warrington, on the West Coast Main Line. There was at one time a station at Moore, which closed in 1943.

An official LNWR photograph of the railway bridge carrying the main line across the Runcorn Gap between Ditton and Liverpool Lime Street, which carried its first passenger train on 1 April 1869. The southern approach to Liverpool had been a long-standing problem for the LNWR. Thirty years after the opening of the GJR, expresses still had to crawl round the sharp curve at Earlestown to meet former L&M metals for access to Lime Street. The GJR did make an attempt to put in a short cut from Moore to Huyton, which would have reduced the distance to the south by 7 miles, but its bill was rejected by Parliament. In 1846, however, powers were obtained to bridge the Runcorn Gap, but they were allowed to elapse because the forceful General Manager of the LNWR, Captain Mark Huish, was more interested in making secret agreements with other railway companies as a way of retaining traffic for his own line, rather than in committing the LNWR to the heavy expenditure needed for the Runcorn Gap project. His wheeler-dealing ensured that there would be insufficient competition to make the project worthwhile. Not until Huish had retired from the LNWR, and the company was able to lease the Warrington–Garston line, were powers again sought to provide a direct line to the south. A bill for a bridge at Fidler's Ferry was strongly opposed, and the LNWR was forced to build the high-level bridge pictured here.

The railway bridge, and transporter bridge, which opened towards the end of the nineteenth century, looking towards Widnes.

The transporter bridge and railway bridge viewed from Victoria Gardens, Widnes.

A panoramic view of the LNWR's Runcorn Gap railway bridge, with the transporter bridge in front. The railway bridge is still in use, carrying Crewe–Liverpool Lime Street electric trains over the gap between Widnes and Runcorn, and justifying the considerable expense of the old Euston company.

Warrington Bank Quay station in the 1920s. Situated on the West Coast Main Line between Crewe and Wigan, the station has been totally rebuilt since the line was electrified to Preston in the late 1960s. Warrington was an early destination on the railway map, when a branch from the Liverpool and Manchester Railway to Dallam Lane was opened in 1831, but the station there was closed in favour of one on the GJR line between Earlestown and Birmingham which opened in July 1837. This station closed in 1868, when Bank Quay was opened. There was also a Warrington Bank Quay Low-Level station, which closed on 9 September 1963, although its Merseyside route remains open for freight. The old low-level line used to carry Liverpool–Manchester passenger trains, but freight trains to Widnes can still be seen passing through. As well as dealing with WCML trains, the station handles trains operating between Chester and Manchester Victoria/Oxford Road, which use the old GWR/LNWR joint line which ran from Birkenhead Woodside to Warrington via Chester General.

An LNWR passenger train for Manchester crosses Stockport Viaduct on its approach to Stockport station. The industrial nature of the town, with factories and mill chimneys clearly visible, can be seen in this view.

Stockport Viaduct under construction in the late nineteenth century. Men involved in its construction pose for the photographer.

Stockport (Edgeley) locoshed on 28 February 1865, with a BR Standard class 2 2–6–2 tank engine in the yard ahead of an 8F 2–8–0, and Hughes-Fowler 'Crab' 2–6–0 No. 42734 on the next road. The shed dealt with local and freight traffic, as its allocation for January 1954 shows:

BR code 9B
Ex-LMS Stanier 2–6–2T: 40071, 40081, 40106, 40138
Ex-LMS Fairburn 2–6–4T: 42120
Ex-LMS Fowler 2–6–4T: 42332, 42353, 42354, 42379
Ex-LMS STanier 2–6–4T: 42445, 42463
Ex-LMS Hughes-Fowler 'Crab' 2–6–0: 42773, 42859, 42934
Ex-LMS 3F 0–6–0: 43281, 43357
Ex-LMS 4F 0–6–0: 44075, 44271, 44340, 44444
Ex-LMS 3F 'Jinty' 0–6–0T: 47289, 47346, 47601
Ex-LNWR 7F 0–8–0: 49010, 49281, 49418, 49453
Total: 27

The ex-LNWR locos were replaced by Stanier 'Black Five' 4–6–0s in the late 1950s, and BR Standard tanks appeared at the shed at around the same time. Stockport was also blessed with another, larger, shed at Heaton Mersey (code 9F).

Close to the southern approaches of Manchester, on the line from Stockport, is Levenshulme station, the exterior of which is seen in this turn-of-the-century view.

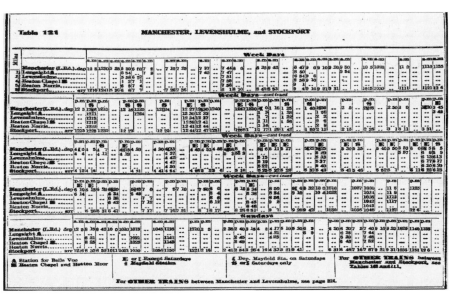

A 1951 BR (LM Region) timetable for local services between Manchester and Stockport, via Levenshulme.

Ex-LMS Stanier 'Mogul' No. 42945 outside Gorton locoshed on 28 February 1965. The shed originally belonged to the Great Central Railway, then the LNER after the Grouping. After nationalization the shed came under Eastern Region control, with the code 39A, but was transferred to the London Midland Region in 1957–8 and recorded 9G; hence its inclusion in this section. The sample allocation included here is for October 1954, when all locos were ex-LNER types.

Ex-LNER Thompson B1 4–6–0: 61161, 61265
Ex-LNER Gresley K3 2–6–0: 61808, 61832, 61865, 61910, 61913, 61966
Ex-GC O4 2–8–0: 63573, 63575, 63582, 63598, 63600, 63603, 63631, 63641, 63681, 63686, 63700, 63709, 63713, 63716, 63719, 63721, 63739, 63743, 63767, 63794, 63805, 63848, 63862, 63895
Ex-GC JK11 0–6–0: 64294, 64298, 64304, 64306, 64311, 64316, 64322, 64326, 64332, 64333, 64342, 64346, 64357, 64363, 64368, 64378, 64382, 64383, 64401, 64409, 64413, 64415, 64426, 64434, 64435, 64437, 64440, 64450
Ex-LNER Gresley J39 0–6–0: 64717, 64718, 64740, 64742, 64743, 64745, 64748
Ex-GC C13 4–4–2T: 67401, 67403, 67405, 67407, 67415, 67417, 67421, 67423, 67425, 67426, 67427, 67431, 67437, 67438, 67440, 67441, 67444, 67445, 67447, 67448, 67450, 67451
Ex-WD J94 0–6–0ST: 68012, 68064, 68079
Ex-LNER Y1 Sentinel four-wheel shunter: 68169
Ex-GC N5 0–6–2T: 69250, 69260, 69270, 69296, 69307, 69308, 69328, 69333, 69338, 69353
Ex-GC A5/1 4–6–2T: 69805, 69806, 69817, 69823, 69829
Total: 108

Gorton shed and yard on 28 February 1965, some seven years after the shed was transferred from Eastern Region to London Midland Region control. Gone are the ex-LNER engines, ex-LMS types, mostly from the now closed Northwich shed, occupying the shed yard. In this view there are both Stanier and Hughes-Fowler 'Moguls' in proliferation. In the foreground is Hughes-Fowler 'Crab' No. 42901, while at its side is Stanier 'Mogul' No. 42974. Gorton had five subsheds, at Ardwick, Dinting, Guide Bridge, Mottram and Reddish, the latter in Stockport, which it retained under LMR control. In its Eastern Region days, Reddish shed was the home of BoBo electric locos Nos 26000–57 and 27000–4, which were used over the Woodhead route, electrified just after the Second World War.

Beeston Castle and Tarporley station exterior, situated about halfway along the Chester and Crewe Railway. The C&CR received royal assent in 1837, just two weeks before the opening of the Grand Junction Railway, and opened to traffic in 1840. The line ran mostly through fields, linking the Roman city of Chester with the railway town of Crewe. It served only small, widely-spaced villages on its 21-mile route through the Cheshire Plain, following the Shropshire Union Canal. Its main engineering feature is the eight-arch viaduct over the River Weaver near Crewe. The original promoters for the line hoped to take the railway into Wales to tap growing traffic to and from Ireland, but the Chester and Holyhead Railway, opened in 1848, later served that market. Three months before opening, the line was absorbed by the GJR to prevent it falling into the hands of its arch rival, the Manchester and Birmingham Railway, which had designs on building lines into the Trent Valley, thereby depriving the GJR of traffic into Birmingham. As it turned out, the M&B line only ever reached Crewe. The line's strategic importance in linking Chester and Crewe has ensured that it remains open today, despite the loss of all its stations, closed in the Beeching years. There has, however, been a suggestion that Beeston Castle and Tarporley station could re-open, an important livestock market operating close to the line at this point.

Table 90 — CHESTER, TATTENHALL, and WHITCHURCH

Miles		Week Days only										Week Days only					
		a.m	a.m	p.m	p.m	p.m	p.m	p.m	p.m	p.m	p.m		a.m	a.m	a.m	p.m	p.m	p.m	p.m
			X	S	W	S	E		E	E	S					S	E	E
—	Chester (General) dep	8 21	1142	1240	1 10	2 14	4 10	5 20	6 10	8 20	10 5	Whitchurch .... dep	7 5	8 10	9 36	1 40	4 12	5 20	6 45
3¾	Waverton	8 8	1148	1246	1 16	..	4 16	5 27	6 21	8 26	1011	Grindley Brook Halt...	7 10	8 15	9 43	1 45	4 17	5 25	6 50
7¾	Tattenhall	8 17	1157	1255	1 25	2 27	4 25	5 36	6 30	8 35	1020	Malpas	7 18	8 23	9 51	1 53	4 25	5 33	6 59
10	Broxton	8 23	12 3	1 1	1 31	2 33	4 31	5 42	6 36	8 41	1027	Broxton	7 25	8 30	9 58	2 0	4 32	5 40	7 6
13¼	Malpas	8 32	1212	1 10	1 40	2 42	4 41	5 52	6 46	8 50	1036	Tattenhall	7 31	8 37	10 4	2 6	4 40	5 49	7 12
—	Grindley Brook Halt.	8 39	1219	1 17	1 47	..	4 48	5 59	6 53	8 57	1043	Waverton.................	7 38	8 45	1011	2 14	4 48	6 1	7 19
20	Whitchurch ...... arr	8 47	1227	1 25	1 55	2 55	4 56	6 7	7 1	9 5	1053	Chester (General).. arr	7 46	8 53	1019	2 22	4 59	6 9	7 31

E Except Saturdays. **S** Saturdays only. **W** Wednesdays only. **X** Except Wednesdays and Saturdays.

For COMPLETE SERVICE between Chester and Waverton, see Table 99.

A timetable for the local service from Chester and along the Whitchurch branch, which was opened by the LNWR in 1872. The 15-mile, double-track line ran from Whitchurch through rural Cheshire to join the Chester and Crewe Railway at Tattenhall Junction. Only a sparse passenger service was ever operated and its last train ran in 1957. Two of the four stations on the line, Malpas and Broxton, were retained for goods use for a further six years and during that time the line was used to test experimental gas turbine loco GT3.

SECTION THREE

Chester

Gateway to the holiday resorts of the north Wales coast, and to the Merseyside docks complexes, Chester was second in importance to Crewe as a major railway junction. Two stations served the town, Chester Northgate (of the Cheshire Lines Committee) and Chester General. The latter was the larger of the two, and was jointly owned by the LNWR and GWR, its status as a joint station being the result of one of the 'great' railway disputes between Captain Mark Huish, the autocratic General Manager of the LNWR and master of the 'dirty trick', who fought hard to drive out all competition to his own railway, and the small but very resilient Shrewsbury and Chester Railway.

Chester began to develop as an important railway junction in the mid-1830s, having attracted the Chester and Birkenhead and Crewe and Chester railways, whose routes met in the city in 1840. The Shrewsbury and Chester Railway entered Chester over the yet incomplete Chester and Holyhead Railway from Saltney Junction in 1846. The Chester and Holyhead Railway reached Chester in 1848, having been given royal assent in 1844.

Both companies at Chester General had their own locosheds, the GWR shed being near the triangle at the northern end of the station, while the larger LNWR shed was beyond the southern end of the station. There was also a locoshed at Chester Northgate, housing Cheshire Lines Committee locos. The LNWR shed closed in the 1960s and a housing estate now occupies the site, while the GWR shed, which closed to steam in the same decade, now houses diesel multiple units and electric multiple units following the three-rail electrification of the Wirral line from Chester to Liverpool Central, which was completed in 1993. The station and locoshed at Chester Northgate also closed in the 1960s; a leisure centre now stands on the site.

Ex-LMS 'Black Five' 4–6–0 No. 45040 waits at platform 10 in Chester General station with an Up train in the mid-1960s. Chester General station was jointly owned by the LNWR/LMS and GWR until nationalization. The LNWR had taken control of the Crewe and Chester in 1846, and the Chester and Holyhead Railway in the 1850s. The company also had a shared interest with the GWR in the line to Birkenhead. The Paddington company gained an interest in Chester thanks to a conflict between the LNWR and its autocratic General Manager, Captain Mark Huish, and the small, but resistant, Shrewsbury and Chester Railway. In 1850 the S&C entered into an agreement with the Shrewsbury and Birmingham Railway over the handling of through traffic between Birmingham and the north-west of England, striking at the heart of the LNWR monopoly. Alarmed by the prospect of competition, Huish issued written threats to the usurpers, with no result. He then decided to use force, by gaining a majority on the management of the station. Once in control, a ban was put on the issue of through tickets to Birmingham via Shrewsbury. He even had the hapless S&C booking clerk physically ejected from the station, and his tickets thrown after him. The Birkenhead, Lancashire and Cheshire Junction Railway, which had become a satellite of the LNWR (but was eventually owned jointly by the LNWR and GWR) was then forced to boycott as much S&C traffic as it could legally dare. Alarmed by the attitude of the LNWR, the Shrewsbury companies began an alliance with the GWR which was interested in reaching Merseyside to take advantage of potential lucrative traffic from the ports there. Huish was eventually defeated in 1854, unwittingly allowing his bitter enemy, the GWR, against whom he had been involved in some major disputes, into Chester. Even when these disputes were settled, bad feeling existed between the two companies for many years, which manifested itself when Chester General station was rebuilt in the 1880s. As if to emphasize their differences, both companies had separate goods facilities at Chester; the LNWR's was to the east of Hoole Road, while the GWR yard was to the west, with approach roads opposite each other.

Both the LNWR and GWR had their own locosheds at Chester. The LNWR's was at the
south end, at the junction of the lines for Crewe and Manchester, and the GWR shed,
the larger of the two, was close to the line to the Wirral and Birkenhead, on the site of
the original LNWR shed. This 1958 view of the GWR shed shows some of its typical
allocation at this time, and includes a 2-6-0 and Hawksworth two-cylinder 'County'
class 4-6-0. Freight to and from the docks at Birkenhead and Paddington–Birkenhead
express motive power was supplied from here. The shed also supplied locos for local
freight and passenger trains, as its allocation for May 1954 shows:

BR code 84K
Hawksworth 'County' class 4-6-0: 1000 *County of Middlesex*, 1008 *County of
Cardigan*, 1022 *County of Northampton*, 1024 *County of Pembroke*
Dean Goods 0-6-0: 2513
Churchward 2-8-0: 2822, 2890, 3820, 3858
Collett 0-6-0PT: 3630, 3665, 3762, 3786, 4602, 5723, 5725, 5748, 5791, 8729, 9728,
9794
Collett 0-6-2T: 5647, 5690
Churchward 2-6-2T: 4115, 4165, 5103, 5174, 5177, 5179, 5186
Churchward 2-6-0: 5311, 5326, 5344, 6331, 6337, 6344, 6345, 6367, 6380, 6392
Collett 'Castle' class 4-6-0: 4076 *Carmarthen Castle*, 5033 *Broughton Castle*, 5061
Earl of Birkenhead, 5075 *Wellington*
Collett 'Hall' class 4-6-0: 5962 *Wantage Hall*, 5968 *Cory Hall*, 6901 *Arley Hall*, 6941
Fillongley Hall, 6963 *Throwley Hall*, 7921 *Edstone Hall*, 7922 *Salford Hall*
Collett 'Grange' class 4-6-0: 6833 *Calcot Grange*, 6835 *Eastham Grange*
Collett 'Manor' class 4-6-0: 7800 *Torquay Manor*, 7801 *Anthony Manor*, 7807
Compton Manor, 7820 *Dinmore Manor*, 7827 *Lydham Manor*
BR class 5 4-6-0: 73020, 73021, 73023, 73024, 73038
Ex-WD 2-8-0: 90214, 90686
Total: 65

The LNWR locoshed and yard in April 1967, with four 'Black Five' 4–6–0s in view. These are No. 45247 of Holyhead shed (6J), No. 45448 of Heaton Mersey (9F), and Chester-allocated Nos 45298 and 44944. The shed's allocation handled freight and local passenger traffic, as its allocation for January 1954 shows:

BR code 6A
Ex-MR 2P 4–4–0: 40377, 40658
Ex-MR 4P 'Compound' 4–4–0: 41106, 41108, 41120, 41121, 41153, 41157, 41158, 41163, 41164, 41166, 41169
Fairburn 2–6–4T: 42063, 42159
Stanier 2–6–4T: 42425, 42450, 42451, 42461, 42540, 42568, 42587, 42595, 42660
Stanier 'Black Five' 4–6–0: 44710, 44910, 45043, 45132, 45180, 45247
3F 'Jinty' 0–6–0T: 47297, 47374, 47375, 47383, 47389, 47504, 47600
BR class 5 4–6–0: 73040, 73041, 73042
Total: 38

The Chester LNWR shed closed in June 1967; a housing estate now occupies the site. Chester also had another locoshed, that of the Cheshire Lines Committee at Northgate (BR code 6D). It had a small allocation of ex-LNER and LMS tank engines, as well as some BR Standard class tender engines. The shed was closed on 21 May 1960.

Chester signals mounted on the Brook Street road overbridge, which gave access to the LNWR goods yard behind the station. These are 'calling-on' signals for access to the goods yard. In the centre and to the right of the picture are the GWR locoshed and goods warehouses. The building with the chevron-pattern front is now used as a depot for modern diesel multiple units and new electric multiple units used on the recently electrified line from Chester to Rock Ferry and Liverpool Central. On the far left is Chester No. 4 signal-box, with the line to Hooton, Rock Ferry and Birkenhead Woodside curving away to the right in the distance.

An underhung bracket signal at Chester station, with the LNWR goods depot behind. Unusually, the left-hand signal arm is fluted, while the right-hand one is plain.

LNWR 4–4–0 No. 1944 at Chester in the early 1920s, just before the Grouping.

Small LNWR 2–4–0 express loco No. 265 at Chester in pre-Grouping days.

LNWR 'Waterloo' class 2–4–0 No. 763 *Violet* at Chester in 1930. Given that it was seven years after the Grouping, the engine still sports its original LNWR number on a cast plate. In the background is the main station building, designed by Francis Thompson in Italianate style with dun-coloured brick and stone facings. It was 1,050 ft long and fronted a 750 ft long platform. The effect of length was offset by the use of pavilions with towers at the corners. The centre two-storey section had all the usual station facilities at ground level, with company offices above. Inside, a 60 ft-span roof was supported opposite the platforms on a brick arcade, behind which stood a large carriage shed. The main building survives today and is still the major feature of the station.

LNWR 'Alfred the Great' class 4–4–0 No. 1974 *Howe* at Chester station around 1920. In the background is the overall station roof, provided when the station was rebuilt in the 1880s, complete with glazed end canopies. After much disagreement between the GWR and LNWR about reconstruction, the new structure followed the classic LNWR large station arrangement employed at places where passenger, parcels, etc, trains were joined and divided. This comprised a small number of long through platforms with central crossover, to facilitate simultaneous use by two trains and remarshalling of stock, plus a number of bays. The Chester extension consisted of, primarily, a large new island platform to the north of the existing station, with an Up line, complete with crossovers on the south side, to match the original single platform that had been the only through platform until the rebuild, and Up and Down through lines on the north side. Two bay platforms were provided at the east end. The first part of the works was brought into use in July 1890 in advance of the rest, in order to assist in the working of summer traffic, which was already considerable by this time.

An ex-MR 2P 4–4–0 on a Manchester-bound train at Chester on 26 August 1953. MR loco types began to appear on what was formerly LNWR territory very soon after the Grouping, the old Derby company being the most influential in the new LMS group, and remained in Chester almost to the end of steam. The glazed end canopies to the overall roof were removed in the early 1950s, and the overall roof itself was demolished in the 1960s. It was replaced with umbrella canopies over the platforms.

The bay platform at the eastern end of Chester station from the passenger foot-bridge, with a BR Standard class 4 4–6–0 at the buffer stops.

LMS 'Black Five' 4–6–0 No. 5151 works its way off shed to collect its train at Chester station on 7 July 1935. At this time the loco would have been virtually new, and Chester locoshed would have been its first home. In the background are the chocolate and cream GWR coaches of the Paddington to Birkenhead express, on the final leg of their journey to Woodside.

The oldest and perhaps most famous express train through Chester was 'The Irish Mail', which was inaugurated in 1848 with the opening of the Chester and Holyhead Railway. It ran between Holyhead and Euston, and was nonstop in LMS days. Here, a relief to the main 'Irish Mail' enters Chester station in the summer of 1951, headed by No. 46140 *King's Royal Rifle Corps*, on its way to Euston. This loco was a member of the 'Royal Scot' class, long associated with the famous train, particularly in un-rebuilt form as shown here. The 'Royal Scots' operated the 'Mail' from 1930 until replaced by BR 'Britannia' Pacifics in 1953. In turn, these were superseded by English-Electric Type 4 diesel-electric locomotives from 1960.

Chester station in the declining years of steam, the mid-1960s. On the centre road is ex-LMS Caprotti valve-geared 'Black Five' No. 44686, one of the last two to be so treated, which has just brought in an excursion train. Its headlamp code is wrong for a light engine. To its left is another example of the class, No. 45093, at the head of another excursion for the north Wales coast, betraying the fact that this is the summer high season, when the station handled several such trains. The station platforms are now covered by the umbrella canopies and the old overall roof has been demolished. Just behind the light engine is the umbrella-style water tank, supplying the still large number of steam locos using the station.

Ex-LMS Stanier 6P5F 2–6–0 No. 42970 passes under the Brook Street roadbridge with a nonstop excursion train from the north Wales coast. This is probably one of the returning holiday trains from Llandudno for Liverpool or Manchester. In steam days, these trains regularly ran through Chester in the peak holiday season.

Another holiday train from the north Wales coast approaches Chester station, headed by an ex-LMS Hughes-Fowler 'Crab' 2–6–0. Almost any type of motive power could be seen at the head of these trains, from 4F 0–6–0 goods engines to 'Jubilee' 4–6–0s, and even ex-LNER B1 class 4–6–0s. In the background an ex-WD 2–8–0 takes a train of open wagons into the old GWR goods yard. Chester No. 4 signal-box can be seen behind the water column at the end of the Down platform.

Ex-LMS Hughes-Fowler 'Crab' 2–6–0 No. 42788 has just been given clearance to take its train forward to the north Wales coast during a 1960s summer. This is almost certainly another holiday train to Llandudno, and has not called at Chester, being on one of the through lines which bypass the platforms.

Freight traffic formed an important part in the activity at Chester station, two companies having goods facilities here. Also, the proximity of the Merseyside docks at Birkenhead meant much freight came through Chester. At the west end of the station, BR 9F 2–10–0 No. 92127 of Crewe North shed (5A) heads a coal train on 5 April 1957.

Ex-LMS Hughes-Fowler 'Crab' 2–6–0 No. 42814 ambles past Chester No. 2 signal-box on its approach to Chester General station, seen almost at a right angle on the left of the picture beyond the signal gantry. The loco is on the main line from Crewe, and the tracks to Manchester are visible beyond the tender. The entrance to the LNWR goods yard is on the right. Several goods vans are in the yard.

An unidentified ex-LMS 'Black Five' brings a fitted freight train of vans past Chester No. 5 signal-box as it heads towards the station from Birkenhead.

A Hughes-Fowler 'Crab' 2–6–0 departs from Chester General station with a Stephenson's Locomotive Society excursion in the early 1950s.

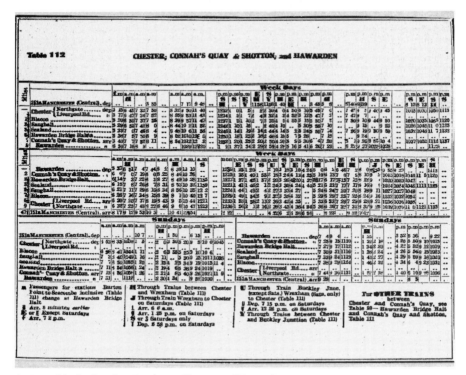

A timetable for local trains from Chester to Hawarden.

A pair of ex-LMS locos in the old LNWR goods yard at Chester. On the left is the front end of Stanier class 5F 'Mogul' No. 42982, while behind is Stanier 8F 2–8–0 No. 48623. Like the ubiquitous 'Black Fives', the 8Fs were a common sight on freight traffic through the station.

Ex-Somerset and Dorset Joint Railway No. 41, a Midland Railway-designed 2P 4–4–0, now LM Region No. 40324, waits beyond Chester General station, having taken on water, some time in 1952. Just visible in the background is the station overall roof and goods vans can be seen at the ex-LNWR warehouse.

The presence of the GWR brought a great variety of motive power to Chester General station. Here, in the early 1960s, is Collett 'Castle' class 4–6–0 No. 7004 *Eastnor Castle*, a BR-built example, backing out of Chester station for the locoshed after bringing in an express from Paddington. The 'Castles' did not appear at Chester until after the Second World War, being thought too heavy for the line between Wolverhampton and Birkenhead. The Paddington–Birkenhead expresses were usually 'King'-hauled as far as the Midlands town, two-cylinder 'Hall' or 'Grange' class 4–6–0s

generally continuing to Chester. As these trains had to reverse at Chester to gain the line to Birkenhead, these locos were taken taken off here and a Prairie tank or 0–6–0 tender engine took the train on to Merseyside. By 1964 ex-GWR locos had disappeared from Chester, ex-LMS 'Black Five' or 'Jubilee' 4–6–0s then operating trains between Birkenhead and Shrewsbury, where 'Western' diesel-hydraulics took over for the run to Paddington.

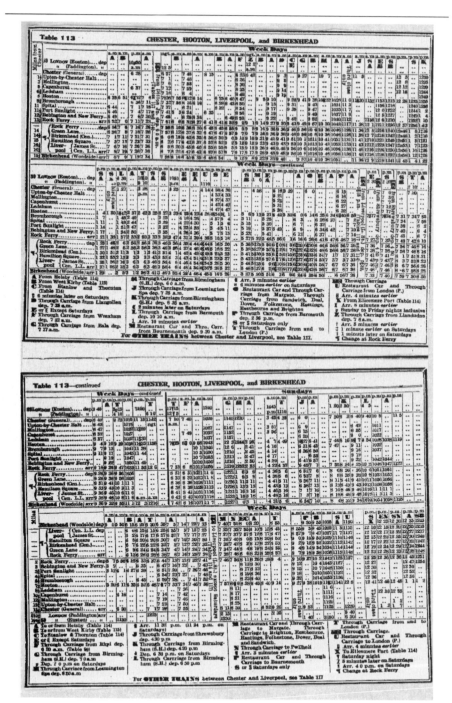

A Western Region timetable for trains operating between Chester and Birkenhead.

Under the overall roof at Chester station in the early 1950s is an interesting contrast in locomotive styles between the GWR and LMS. On the left is ex-GWR Churchward-designed 2–6–2 Prairie tank No. 5179, while behind and to the right is ex-LMS Stanier-designed 2–6–2 tank No. 40110. The GWR loco is at the head of a train for Birkenhead, while the LMS loco waits in the centre road for its next turn of duty. The photograph appears to have been taken in the summer as the station seems to be busy with day-trippers and holiday-makers.

An evening photograph, taken in the early 1950s, of Hawksworth 'County' class 4–6–0 No. 1025 *County of Radnor*. The loco appears to have just brought in the Shrewsbury–Chester section of the Paddington–Birkenhead express.

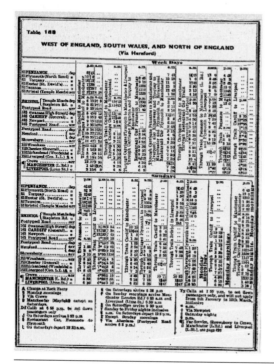

A GWR timetable for expresses between Birkenhead, the south-west of England and south Wales via Chester.

On 17 May 1964 a Stanier 2–6–4 tank waits to take over the express from Paddington to Birkenhead. By this time these trains were in the hands of ex-LMS locos between Shrewsbury and Birkenhead, a 4–6–0 bringing the train as far as Chester, from where the 2–6–4 tanks took over for the run to Merseyside. In the background, the main line to the north Wales coast can be seen curving away to the left, beyond the rake of passenger coaches. The lines to north Wales and Birkenhead were joined by a direct line, thereby avoiding a run into the station and a reverse. This triangle later proved useful for turning steam locos which were used for special excursions after the general demise of such traction in the late 1960s.

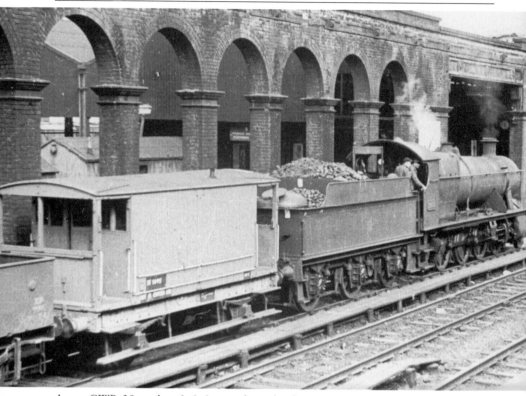

An ex-GWR 28xx class 2–8–0 runs through Chester station with a freight train in the late 1950s. Behind the train are the arches that once supported the overall roof, long since demolished. The arches remain today as an integral part of the present station.

An ex-GWR clerestory corridor coach in September 1950. This must surely be the only GW clerestory coach to be painted in BR red and cream. Note that the coach number is painted at the 'wrong' end.

The Northgate Tunnels at Chester, which carried the main lines to Holyhead and Shrewsbury below the old CLC line to Northwich.

Table 153— *continued*

CHESTER, SHREWSBURY, WOLVERHAMPTON, BIRMINGHAM, and LONDON

Miles from Chester	Week Days	p.m	am	a.m	a.m		am	a.m	a.m	a.m	a.m	a.m	a.m		a.m	a.m	a.m	a.m	a.m	a.m	a.m	a.m
	L M R MANCHESTER (Exch.) dep	1020	..	..	..	..	..	..	..	..	..	..	..	..	..	..	..	..	..	..	..	..
	WARRINGTON (B. Q.) "	1058	..	..	..	..	..	..	..	..	..	..	..	..	..	..	..	..	..	..	..	..
	LIVERPOOL (Cen. L.L.)¶ "	11 5	..	..	..	..	..	..	..	..	..	..	..	..	..	..	..	..	..	..	..	6 15
	BIRKENHEAD (W'side) "	1115	..	..	..	..	..	..	..	..	..	..	..	..	..	..	..	..	..	..	..	6 30
—	Chester (General) dep	1220	..	..	..	..	..	..	..	..	..	..	..	..	..	..	..	..	..	..	..	7 10
2¼	Saltney	a.m	..	..	..	..	..	..	..	..	..	..	..	..	..	..	..	..	..	..	..	7 14
4	Balderton	..	..	..	..	..	..	..	..	..	..	..	..	..	..	..	..	..	..	..	..	..
7½	Rossett	..	..	..	..	..	..	..	..	..	..	..	..	..	..	..	..	..	..	..	..	..
9	Gresford (for Llay)	..	..	..	..	..	..	..	Ⓐ	..	..	..	..	..	..	..	..	..	..	..	..	..
12¼	Wrexham	1248	..	..	..	..	..	..	6 35	..	..	..	..	..	..	..	..	..	..	7 3	..	7 32
15½	Johnstown and Hafod	..	..	..	..	..	..	..	6 40	..	..	..	..	..	..	..	..	..	..	7 9	..	..
16½	Wynnville Halt	..	..	..	..	..	..	..	6 43	..	..	..	..	..	..	..	..	..	..	..	..	..
—	187 PWLLHELI dep	5‖40	..	..	..	..	..	..	..	..	..	..	..	..	..	..	..	..	..	..	..	..
—	187 BARMOUTH "	7‖20	..	..	..	..	..	..	..	..	..	..	..	..	..	..	..	..	..	..	..	..
17	Ruabon	1J0	..	..	..	..	..	..	6 47	..	..	..	..	..	TC Shrewsbury to Paddington	..	Wolverhampton to Oxford. On Saturdays, commencing 27th May will run to Portsmouth Harbour, arr. 1 39 p.m. (Tables 152 and 83)	..	..	7 13	..	7 45
18¼	Rhosymedre Halt	Except Mondays	..	..	..	..	..	..	6 50	..	..	..	..	..	..	..	..	..	..	..	..	..
18¾	Cefn	..	..	..	..	..	..	..	6 52	..	..	..	..	..	..	..	..	..	..	..	..	7 50
19¾	Whitehurst	..	..	..	..	..	..	..	6 55	..	..	..	..	..	..	..	..	..	..	To Barmouth (Table 187)	..	..
21¼	Chirk	..	..	..	..	..	..	..	6 59	..	..	..	..	..	..	..	..	..	..	..	..	7 55
22¼	Trehowell Halt	..	..	..	..	..	..	..	..	..	..	..	..	..	..	..	..	..	..	..	..	..
22¾	Weston Rhyn	..	..	..	..	..	..	..	7 3	..	..	..	..	..	..	..	..	..	..	..	..	..
24¼	Gobowen arr	1J13	..	..	..	..	..	..	7 7	..	..	..	..	..	..	..	..	..	..	..	..	8 2
26½	158 Oswestry arr	..	..	..	..	..	..	..	7 18	..	..	..	..	..	..	..	..	..	..	..	..	8 15
	dep	10‖25	..	..	..	..	..	..	..	..	..	..	..	..	..	..	..	..	..	..	..	7 50
—	Gobowen dep	..	..	..	..	..	..	..	..	..	..	..	..	..	..	..	..	..	..	..	..	8 3
26½	Whittington (Low Level)	..	..	..	..	..	..	..	..	..	..	..	..	..	..	..	..	..	..	..	..	..
29½	Rednal and West Felton	..	..	..	..	..	..	..	..	..	Restaurant Car Train Wolverhampton to Paddington	..	..	..	Buffet Car from Wolverhampton	..	..	..	..	..	..	TC Birkenhead to Paddington
30½	Haughton Halt	..	..	..	..	..	..	..	..	..	..	..	..	..	..	..	..	..	..	..	..	..
33¼	Stanwardine Halt	..	..	..	..	..	..	..	..	..	..	..	..	..	..	..	..	..	..	..	..	..
34¼	Baschurch	..	..	..	..	..	..	..	..	..	..	..	..	..	..	..	..	..	..	..	..	8 18
37	Oldwoods Halt	..	..	..	..	..	..	..	..	..	..	..	..	..	..	..	..	..	..	..	..	..
38½	Leaton	..	..	..	..	..	..	..	..	..	..	..	..	..	..	..	..	..	..	..	..	8 24
42½	Shrewsbury arr	1 35	..	..	..	..	..	..	..	..	..	..	..	..	..	..	..	..	..	..	..	8 31
—	184 ABERYSTWYTH dep	..	..	..	..	..	..	..	..	..	..	..	..	..	..	..	..	..	..	..	..	..
—	184 WELSHPOOL "	..	..	..	..	..	..	..	..	..	..	..	..	..	..	..	..	..	..	..	..	..
—	Shrewsbury dep	..	..	..	..	..	..	..	..	..	..	..	6 35	..	7 25	7 55	..	8 0	..	..	..	8 37
46½	Upton Magna	..	..	..	..	..	..	..	..	..	..	..	6 43	..	..	..	..	8 7	..	..	..	..
48¾	Walcot	..	..	..	..	..	..	..	..	..	..	..	6 48	..	..	..	..	8 12	..	..	..	..
51	Admaston	..	..	..	..	..	..	..	..	..	..	..	6 53	..	..	..	..	8 16	..	..	..	..
—	159 MANCHESTER (L. Rd.) dep	..	..	..	..	..	..	..	..	..	..	..	..	..	1230	..	..	..	..	..	..	..
—	159 CREWE "	..	..	..	..	..	..	..	..	..	..	..	..	..	6 5	..	..	..	..	..	..	..
52¾	Wellington	..	..	..	..	..	..	TC Wolverhampton to Paddington	..	..	..	6 35	7r 2	..	7 42	8 10	..	8 21	..	..	8 30	8 55
54¼	New Hadley Halt	..	..	..	..	..	..	..	..	..	..	6 40	7 6	..	..	..	..	..	..	..	8 34	..
55¼	Oakengates	..	..	..	..	..	..	..	..	..	..	6 50	7 13	..	7 49	..	..	..	..	..	8 38	..
59¼	Shifnal	..	..	..	..	..	..	..	..	..	Except Saturdays	7 0	7 24	..	7 57	..	..	..	..	..	8 46	..
63	Cosford	..	..	..	..	..	..	..	..	..	..	7 8	7 32	..	8 4	..	..	..	8 21	..	8 52	9 10
64½	Albrighton	..	..	..	..	..	..	..	..	..	..	7 12	7 36	..	..	..	..	..	8 25	..	8 56	..
67½	Codsall	..	..	..	..	..	..	..	..	..	..	7 20	7 43	..	8 13	..	..	..	8 33	..	9 2	..
68½	Birches and Bilbrook Halt	..	..	..	..	..	..	..	..	..	..	7 23	7 46	..	..	..	..	..	8 36	..	9 5	..
71¼	Dunstall Park	..	..	..	..	..	..	..	..	..	..	7 29	7 53	..	..	..	..	..	8 42	..	9 12	..
72¾	Wolverhampton (Low Level) arr	..	..	..	..	..	..	..	..	..	..	7 32	7 56	..	8 23	..	..	..	8 45	..	9 15	9 28
	dep	..	520	5 40	6 5	..	625	6 45	..	6 58	7 10	7 44	8 3	..	8 33	..	8 42	..	..	..	..	9 35
74¼	Priestfield	..	..	5 44	6 9	..	629	..	..	7 2	..	7 48	8 7	..	..	..	..	..	..	..	..	..
75¾	Bilston	..	528	5 48	6 13	..	633	6 52	..	7 6	7 16	7 52	8 11	..	..	..	8 48	..	..	..	..	..
77½	Wednesbury	..	533	5 53	6 18	..	639	6 58	..	7 12	7 22	7 57	8 16	..	..	..	8 53	..	..	..	..	..
79	Swan Village	..	537	5 57	6 22	..	644	..	..	7 16	..	8 2	8 21	..	..	..	8 58	..	..	..	..	..
80	West Bromwich	..	542	6 2	6 27	..	649	..	..	7 20	7 30	8 6	8 26	..	..	..	9 2	..	..	..	..	..
82	Handsworth and Smethwick	..	546	6 6	6 32	..	654	..	..	7 25	7 35	8 11	8 31	..	..	..	9 7	..	..	..	..	..
83	Soho and Winson Green	..	549	6 9	6 35	..	657	..	..	7 28	..	8 14	8 34	..	..	..	9 10	..	..	..	..	..
83¾	Hockley	..	552	6 12	6 38	..	7 0	..	..	7 31	..	8 17	8 37	..	..	..	9 13	..	..	..	..	..
84¾	Birmingham (Snow Hill) arr	..	555	6 15	6 41	..	7 4	7 14	..	7 35	7 43	8 20	8 41	..	8 55	..	9 16	..	..	..	..	9 55
108	152 LEAMINGTON SPA arr	..	..	7 19	..	..	..	7 55	..	..	8 31	..	..	..	9 27	..	9 47	..	..	..	..	1027
130½	152 OXFORD "	..	..	..	..	..	..	9 5	..	..	..	..	..	..	..	..	1050	..	..	..	..	12 5
178	152 READING GENERAL "	..	..	..	..	..	..	10 2	..	..	..	..	..	..	..	..	1138	..	..	..	..	..
195½	152 PADDINGTON "	..	..	..	..	..	..	10 5	..	..	1015	..	..	..	1120	..	1225	..	..	..	..	1225

J Calls to set down passengers only
‖ p.m. Via Wrexham
r Arr. 6 57 a.m.
TC Through Carriages
¶ Change at Rock Ferry
Ⓐ Third class only

A GWR timetable for expresses between Birkenhead and Paddington.

SECTION FOUR

Lines to the Wirral

Rather ironically, given events at Chester, the main line serving the Wirral, between Birkenhead Woodside and Warrington via Chester General, was vested jointly in the LNWR/LMS and GWR, the latter company using the section between Chester and Birkenhead as its main line, thereby linking Paddington with Merseyside, in competition with the Euston–Liverpool Lime Street route of the LNWR. Access to Liverpool from Woodside was via the old Woodside Ferry, still operating today.

Other lines serving the Wirral included the Wirral Railway between Hooton and New Brighton, a popular resort on the Mersey estuary, many Liverpudlians arriving there by train or Mersey ferry for a day out during the summer months. There was also the Mersey Railway which passed under the Mersey to reach Liverpool from the main Woodside line at Rock Ferry. Another line into the Wirral was the Great Central line from Wrexham to Seacombe. Following the Grouping, this line provided the LNER with its only route into Wales.

The Wirral also had an important junction station at Hooton, where all lines, except the Seacombe–Wrexham line, met. From Hooton, one other line, that to Helsby, provided a connection between the Wirral and the main line from Chester to Warrington and Manchester. Only the line between Hooton and Helsby via Ellesmere Port and the old Woodside line as far as Rock Ferry still exist, the latter line now being part of the route to Liverpool Central, having been fully electrified since 1993.

Ex-GWR Collett 'Grange' class 4–6–0 No. 6844 *Penhydd Grange* of Birkenhead shed (6C) makes ready to depart from Birkenhead Woodside station with a local service for Chester in 1952. Birkenhead Woodside represented the GWR's final success in reaching the Mersey. Ironically, this was only achieved by joint ownership of the line from Chester through the Wirral to Birkenhead with the Paddington company's bitter enemy, the LNWR. Woodside was important to the GWR because there was a direct ferry service across the Mersey to Liverpool. The line between Chester and Birkenhead was opened by the Chester and Birkenhead Railway in 1840, with a terminus at Grange Lane serving three ferries which then operated out of Birkenhead. By October 1844 an extension of ¾ mile was opened from Grange Lane via a 400 yd tunnel (pictured here) to a new station, which was to become Birkenhead Woodside, Merseyside's first riverside station. At high tide the distance between trains and boats could be as little as 50 yd. A unique feature of the station was that the original main entrance was destined not to be used by passengers, a side door being adopted for the purpose when the local tramway set up its terminus nearby. The CBR was taken over by the Birkenhead, Lancashire and Cheshire Junction Railway on 22 July 1847, the line between Birkenhead and Warrington via Chester becoming the Birkenhead Railway in August 1859. From 20 November 1860 the BR was vested jointly in the GWR and LNWR (after Captain Mark Huish of the LNWR had left the Euston Company), and through passenger expresses between Paddington and Birkenhead began on 1 October 1861. The station at Woodside was closed on 6 November 1967, and the station site is now occupied by an office block, Great Western House, which houses the headquarters of the north-western division of the controversial Child Support Agency.

A GWR Churchward Mogul passes through Hooton station with a train of open goods wagons for Chester. Although a through station, all local trains terminated here, except for those operating between Birkenhead and Chester. The station was an important Wirral junction serving lines to Kirby and Helsby, and survives today, with electric trains operating through the station between Chester and Liverpool Central via Rock Ferry, the latter point being where the Mersey Railway once commenced. The MR was steam-operated until it was electrified in 1902. The GWR operated a steam service from Paddington to Liverpool Central from 1898, using the Mersey Railway for access to Liverpool. This service ceased when the line between Rock Ferry and Liverpool was electrified.

A January 1950 timetable for local services between Birkenhead and Chester.

The station and signal-box at Ellesmere Port, on the line between Hooton and Helsby, in the 1930s. This line, like that between Chester and Birkenhead, was jointly operated by the GWR and LNWR/LMS. Ellesmere Port was an important industrial area which was served by canal until the opening of the railway in 1863. The line is still in use today, operated by a DMU service, and Ellesmere Port has a major role as an oil-refining centre.

Helsby station, terminus of the branch from Hooton via Ellesmere Port. At this point the branch joins the main line from Chester to Warrington Bank Quay. This view shows the station on the main line, the branch terminating behind the signal-box at the far end of the station.

114   **HOOTON and HELSBY**

Week Days ... **Sundays**

...dep									
Sutton									
...mere Port									
...w and Thornton									
...nd Elton									
...y	arr								

Week Days ... **Sundays**

...y	dep								
...nd Elton									
...w and Thornton									
...mere Port									
Sutton									
...n	arr								

A Third class only. ✓ **S** Saturdays only. **S** From Birkenhead (Table 113). **$** Arrive 5 minutes earlier. **C** From Rock Ferry (Table 113).
D Through Carriage Liverpool (Lime St.) dep. 6 32 a.m to Hooton **E** Except Saturdays. **F** To Birkenhead (Table 113).
Arrive 10 9 p.m. **M** To Rock Ferry (Table 113). **Z** From Birkenhead except on Saturdays (Table 113)

A 1950 timetable for trains along the Hooton–Helsby branch.

Continuing along the main line from Helsby, in the direction of Warrington, lies the station at Frodsham, which could once boast a large sidings complex and signal-box, though both had gone by the mid-1960s. The line through Frodsham was always busy with passenger traffic between north Wales and Manchester via Warrington Bank Quay, along with freight from Manchester to the John Summers steelworks at Shotton on the Chester and Holyhead line, and traffic to Ellesmere Port oil and chemical works.

Late nineteenth-century Mickle Trafford station on the joint line between Chester and Warrington. The station lay between Chester and Helsby and was a very simple structure, judging by this view. It was provided with a staff of three, who are posed at the Chester end of the station. The Cheshire Lines Committee's route between Northwich and Chester Northgate created a junction here, which was completed in 1878, having been authorized on 5 July 1875. The station no longer exists.

The simple wooden station at West Kirby, on the joint line from Hooton, close to the Wirral Railway line to New Brighton. Like the rest of the line from Hooton, it was closed in the 1960s, and only a local footpath acts as a reminder that trains ever operated here.

West Kirby station on the Wirral Railway. The electric railway here served an expanding residential area, and linked the Wirral with Liverpool via Birkenhead. The station was a substantial brick structure complete with turreted clock tower.

Table 110 — LIVERPOOL (CEN., L.L.) and BIRKENHEAD to NEW BRIGHTON and WEST KIRBY

A timetable for train services over the Wirral Railway.

105

Heswall station, on the Great Central Railway between Bidston and Wrexham Central. The line opened on 18 May 1896 and became part of the LNER after the 1923 Grouping, giving the King's Cross company its only line into Wales. In this view, a Great Central Railway tank loco heads a train from Bidston to Wrexham into the smart, substantial station. The line is still open, operating a DMU service between Wrexham and the 'Merseyrail' service to Liverpool.

What appears to be a rush-hour train at Heswall station, with a large number of passengers alighting.

A timetable for services between Seacombe and Wrexham on the old Great Central line.

A symbol of the decline of British railways. Thurstaston station, on the line between Hooton and West Kirby, lies derelict after closure in the 1960s. The area around the old station has now become part of the Wirral Country Park, established in 1969. Thurstaston is now the site of a visitor centre.

Table 115 — HOOTON and WEST KIRBY

Week Days

	a.m	a.m	a.m	a.m	a.m a.m					p.m	p.m p.m		p.m p.m	Sundays
Hooton ....dep	6 20	6 51	7 22	8 13	10 39 11 35	1 4	2 53	2 50	3 41	4 48 5 54	5 8	7 40 9 10	..
Hadlow Road........	..	7 0	7 27	8 19	10 34 11 39	1 9	1 59	2 54	3 45	4 54 5 56	6 18	7 45 9 16	..
Neston	6 30	7 6	7 33	8 24	10 41 11 2	1 15	2 5	3 0	3 51	5 0 6 4	6 25	7 51 9 23	..
Parkgate	6 35	7 10	7 42	8 27	10 45 11 6	1 18	2 10	3 4	3 55	5 4 6 9	6 29	7 56 9 26	..
Heswall............	6 44	7 20	7 45	8 33	10 51 11 13	1 25	2 15	3 6	4 0	5 8 6 14	6 33	8 0 9 31	..
Thurstaston........	6 52	7 28	8 0	8 40	10 57 11 18	1 28	2 20	3 14	4 5	5 13 6 19	6 38	8 6 9 36	..
Caldy	..	..	8 4	8 44	11 1 ..	1 32	..	3 18	4 9	5 17 6 23	..	..	..
Kirby Park	..	..	7 57	8 47	11 4 11 22	1 36	2 27	3 22	4 13	5 21 6 26	..	..	..
West Kirby ....arr	7 0	7 40	8 10	8 50	11 7 11 29	1 39	2 30	3 25	4 16	5 24 6 29	6 47	8 15 9 45	..

Week Days

	a.m	a.m	a.m a.m	a.m	a.m				p.m	p.m p.m		p.m p.m	Sundays
West Kirby .....dep	6 17	7 19	7 50 8 20	9 0	.. 11 17	12 40	2 0	2 49	3 4 26	3 47 4 51	6 56 6 25	..
Kirby Park	..	7 21	7 52 8 22	..	11 19	..	2 2	2 47	3 27	4 27 4 53	6 56	..
Caldy	..	..	7 56 8 25	9 4	11 22	..	2 5	..	3 40	4 30 5 26	..	..
Thurstaston........	6 25	7 26	7 59 8 30	9 8	11 26	12 46	2 8	2 54 3 44	3 43 4 44	4 34 5 37	7 0 7 5 8 36	..
Heswall............	6 30	7 33	8 4 8 44	9 13	11 31	12 52	2 16	2 59 3 50	4 30	4 39 5 37	7 10	..
Parkgate	6 35	7 38	8 9 8 49	9 18	11 36	12 56	2 21	3 4 53	4 44	4 44 5 41	7 15 8 47	..
Neston	6 39	7 42	8 13 8 53	9 22	11 40	1 2 25	..	3 10 4 1	4 46	6 13 7 18	7 19 8 52	..
Hadlow Road........	6 44	7 46	8 16 8 59	9 26	11 46	1 6 30	..	3 15 4 7	4 53	6 18 7 24	7 24 8 57	..
Hooton ....arr	6 49	7 52	8 23 9 3	9 32	11 50	1 13 36	..	3 20 4 12	4 58	6 27 7 28	7 29 9 1	..

B From Birkenhead (Table 113).   s Arr. 6 mins. earlier.   E Except Saturdays.   F To Birkenhead (Table 113).   S Saturdays only.
U From Birkenhead on Saturdays (Table 113).   V To Birkenhead on Saturdays (Table 113)

In better days, a timetable for local services between Hooton and West Kirby, the line on which Thurstaston station once stood.

SECTION FIVE

Cheshire Lines Committee

Although it was little known outside the county, the Cheshire Lines Committee route was one of the most important joint lines in Britain. However, contrary to its title, its busiest lines were in the cotton mill areas of south Lancashire.

The CLC had three partners, the Great Northern Railway, the Manchester, Sheffield and Lincolnshire Railway (later to become the Great Central Railway) and the Midland Railway. The first two were to become part of the LNER at the 1923 Grouping, bringing east coast locomotives to the north-west of England, while the Midland Railway became part of the LMS at the same time. All three companies provided motive power for CLC trains. The Committee inherited a line between Chester and Northwich, which had been conceived by three small companies, although it was not then operational. The Cheshire Midland Company, as the CLC was then known, was formed in 1860, at a time when a revival in the salt industry, for which the area was famous, was forecast, to complete a 13-mile line from Manchester South Junction and Altrincham to Northwich. Altrincham and Knutsford were linked in 1862, and Northwich was reached by the beginning of the following year. The section between Northwich and Chester was not completed until 1874. The company established a terminus at Chester, known as Northgate station, and a locoshed was also sited there. Its principal passenger services were between Northgate and Manchester Central via Northwich, along with services between Chester and Wrexham. The small locoshed contained a dozen or so ex-LNER engines in 1947, but these had been diluted with ex-LMS tank locos and freight engines, along with BR Standard classes of tender engines by the late 1950s.

The CLC main line passed largely through rural Cheshire, but was always important for freight traffic, and it linked many mid-Cheshire towns. By the 1960s services had been run down, and the locoshed at Northgate was closed on 21 May 1960. Chester Northgate station closed on 6 October 1969, and the site is now occupied by the Northgate Leisure Centre. Despite the loss of its Chester base, the CLC line between Altrincham and Mouldsworth remains open to passengers, trains now terminating at Chester General station. The line is still important for freight, as it serves the oil refineries at Ellesmere Port.

Delamere station on the CLC line between Chester Northgate and Manchester Central, with ex-Great Central Railway and LNER class C13 4–4–2 tank on an RCTS railtour in 1953. The loco would have been one of those allocated to Chester Northgate locoshed (BR code 6D), and only two coaches make up the train. The section of the line between Northwich and Helsby (where it joined the Birkenhead Railway) was fully opened in 1869, having been incorporated in 1861. From Helsby the line veered northwards from a direct approach to Chester at Mouldsworth. It was left to the CLC as inheritor of the powers of the West Cheshire Railway (which had built the earlier section of the line) to complete the route from Mouldsworth to Chester Northgate, which opened in 1874.

Winsford and Over station, at the end of the 6 mile branch from Cuddington, between Delamere and Hartford, in 1954. The CLC claimed that, along with Knutsford and Northwich, it was the most important town the company served. The branch meandered through wooded country and had several crossings before reaching the modest terminus of a single platform and a few sidings. There was only one intermediate stop, at Whitegate. The branch was not built primarily for passengers, but for salt, the line serving eight busy salt works. The branch was authorized in 1862 and opened to traffic eight years later. Passenger services were withdrawn after only four years, but were restored twice before being withdrawn for good after one of the first legal battles over road and rail competition. The battle began after the CLC announced withdrawal of passenger services from 1 January 1931, the LMS stating that buses would provide an alternative link. A few months later Winsford Council went to court to take advantage of a ruling made after the original closure of the line to passengers in 1874. Services had been resumed in 1886, but after an accident the Board of Trade banned passenger workings until £7,500 had been spent on interlocking points and signals. Unwilling to pay, the CLC halted passenger services. The Local Board complained to the Railway Commissioners, who ordered the CLC to operate passenger trains. This ruling ensured passenger services from 1892 until 1930, when the CLC presented evidence of decline in answer to the council's application. Between 1924 and 1930, passenger numbers had fallen from 99,000 to 68,000 and receipts from £1,700 to £800. The council's case was finally rejected, and passenger services were not restored. The line closed in 1958.

The substantial station at Hartford and Greenbank in 1953, with C13 4–4–2T No. 67436 leading an RCTS railtour. Quite a crowd are on the platform, most being passengers on the excursion.

The entrance to the important CLC station at Northwich. The town is the centre of one of the richest salt deposits in Britain, and to capture salt traffic being carried on local rivers and canals, a network of branch lines was built which extended some 5 miles. These lines were opened in 1867, and followed three years later by another between Hartford and Winnington, the descent to the terminus, at 1 in 53, giving the CLC its steepest gradient. The LNWR also had access to Northwich via a north-to-east spur (Northwich to Sandbach and Crewe) which opened in 1870.

Another view of Northwich station entrance, showing the substantial building which befitted such an important location. Several carriages appear in this scene, along with an early motorcar. It was the invention of the car that was to do so much damage to the railways, although nobody realized it at the time.

Table 151a — MANCHESTER (Central) NORTHWICH, and CHESTER

Week Days / Sundays

Station list (downward):
Manchester (Central) dep., Old Trafford, Stretford, Sale, Altrincham & Bowdon, Ashley, Mobberley, Knutsford, Plumley, Lostock Gralam, Northwich, Hartford and Greenbank, Cuddington, Mouldsworth, Barrow, for Tarvin, Mickle Trafford, Chester (Northgate) arr., Wrexham (Gen.) arr.

Station list (upward):
Wrexham (Gen.) dep., Mickle Trafford, Barrow, for Tarvin, Mouldsworth, Delamere, Cuddington, Hartford and Greenbank, Northwich, Lostock Gralam, Knutsford, Mobberley, Sale, Altrincham & Bowdon arr., Sale, Stretford, Old Trafford, Manchester (Central) arr.

A — Arr. 3 56 p.m. on Saturdays.   B — Arr. 6 mins. earlier.   C — Arr. 12 59 p.m. on Saturday.
D — Dep. 1 25 p.m. on Saturdays.   S or S — Saturdays only.   E or F — Except Saturdays.   P — Arr. 12 59 p.m. on Saturday.
T — Dep. 3 48 p.m. on Saturdays.   Z — Arr. 5 mins. earlier.

For LOCAL TRAINS between Manchester and Altrincham and Bowdon, see Table 122
For OTHER TRAINS between Manchester and Chester, see Table 99—
Mickle Trafford and Chester, Table 117

A timetable of January 1950 for passenger services over the CLC route between Chester Northgate and Manchester Central.

114

An unidentified ex-Midland Railway loco at the head of a train at Northwich station. Several rakes of passenger rolling stock are also present. As an important intermediate destination, with several branches meeting here, Northwich was provided with a locoshed (coded 8E in BR days, being part of London Midland Region). Its allocation was largely made up of ex-LNER types including GC 'Director' class 4–4–0s, J10 0–6–0s, L3 2–6–4 tanks, N5 0–6–2 tanks and 04 2–8–0 goods engines. There were also some ex-LMS types, including 8F 2–8–0s, which were allocated to Northwich for use on limestone trains from Buxton to the ICI works in the town. The shed was closed in the early 1960s, though the shed building remained *in situ* and was still standing in the mid-1980s.

A busy platform scene at Northwich station, the clock showing 10 o'clock. All the station staff are posing for the photograph, and a family is waiting for a train to go on holiday, judging by the Sunday-best dress of mother and child, and the luggage on the porter's trolley.

Another view of Northwich station, at 10.30 a.m. A rake of CLC passenger coaches can be seen at the opposite platform.

As the CLC reached the outer residential suburbs of Manchester, the stations became large, as seen in this view of Hale. The station appears to have a strong Midland Railway influence, the company being one of the partners of the CLC. The station has its fair share of advertisements, and a covered foot-bridge linking the platforms gives some idea of its importance in the CLC network.

The exterior of Altrincham and Bowden station, complete with carriages awaiting the arrival of a train. The clock is showing 1.55 p.m.; perhaps a train is due at 2 o'clock.

Some of the local population posing outside Altrincham and Bowden station. The carriages give an impression of what a 'well-to-do' area Altrincham was, and still is.

From 11 May 1931 an electric service using the 1,500 V d.c. overhead contact system was introduced between Altrincham and Manchester, especially for commuter traffic into the city. Here, the interior of Altrincham station can be seen, complete with overhead wires for the electric services.

One of the electric multiple units, introduced in 1931, running between Manchester and Altrincham.

Another view of the platforms at Altrincham station on a dull, wet day in the 1950s.

A modern view of Altrincham station, with a 25 kV a.c. electric multiple unit approaching. Changeover to this new form of traction was completed between Crewe and Manchester in 1960.

CHESHIRE LINES.

Easter Holiday Excursions

On GOOD FRIDAY, SATURDAY, SUNDAY and EASTER MONDAY,

APRIL 14th, 15th, 16th and 17th, 1922,

DAY EXCURSION TICKETS will be issued to

CHESTER

(NORTHGATE STATION), as under:—

STATIONS.	GOOD FRIDAY and EASTER SUNDAY	SATURDAY		EASTER MONDAY		Fare to Chester and Back. ONE DAY. Third Class.
	A.M.	A.M.	P.M.	A.M.	P.M.	
MANCHESTER (Central) .... dep.	10 0	10 0	1 30	9 30	1 15	**5/-**
CHESTER (Northgate) ...... arr.	11 45	11 40	3 15	11 15	3 0	

Children under Three years of age, Free ; Three and under Twelve, Half-Fares.

The Day Tickets will be available for returning from CHESTER (Northgate Station) on Good Friday and Easter Sunday at 7 45 p.m., on Saturday and Easter Monday at 6 40 and 8 0 p.m.

SATURDAY TO MONDAY TICKETS—

CHEAP WEEK-END TICKETS are issued between any Two Stations, available on the Outward Journey on Saturdays by any Train, and to return on Sundays by any Train after 6 0 a.m. (where Train Services permit), and on Mondays by any Train, at a **SINGLE FARE AND A THIRD** (plus fractions of 3d.) **FOR THE DOUBLE JOURNEY.**

MINIMUM :—FIRST CLASS, 10/- ; THIRD CLASS 5/-.

For full particulars apply at the Company's Stations, Agents, and Town Offices.

Excursion Tickets.—Excursion tickets are not transferable, and are available only to and from the stations named upon them, and by the trains named in the Company's Bills, etc., announcing the excursion, and if used to or from any station beyond, or short of, the stations named on the tickets, or by any trains not advertised in the bills, &c., they will be forfeited, and the holders thereof will be charged the full ordinary fare for the whole distance travelled.   NO LUGGAGE ALLOWED.

IMPORTANT NOTICE.—Tickets may be had at the Stations any time in advance, and in Manchester and District at the Agents' Offices shewn below :—Messrs. T. Cook & Son, 77, Market Street, Victoria Bridge, and Midland Hotel ; Messrs. Dean & Dawson, 53, Piccadilly ; Messrs. Swan & Leach, 27, Princess Street, and 212, Stretford Road ; Mr. Frank Short, Tower Entrance, Royal Exchange Mr. A. Carter, 152, Alexandra Road and 6, Oldham Road, New Cross ; Great Central Railway Co., 3, ansgate ; Midland Railway Co., 47, Piccadilly ; Mr. J. Gibson, 337, Regent Road, Salford.

Central Station, Liverpool, March, 1922.   **JOHN E. CHARNLEY, Manager.**

C. TINLING & CO., LTD., Printing Contractors, 55, Victoria Street, Liverpool.   No. 47

The CLC worked hard to attract passengers to its line, and often ran special excursions on bank holiday weekends. Here, the Committee is advertising a day excursion from Manchester to Chester during the 1922 Easter weekend for 5s (25p).

As well as its line from Chester to Manchester, the CLC had a route between Liverpool Central and Manchester Central. One of the stations on that route was at Glazebrook, pictured here.

Along with Bank Quay, Warrington also had a CLC station, known as Warrington Central. The station lay on what was formerly a loop from the direct Manchester–Liverpool line, and was opened on 1 August 1873. It comprised two long platforms, seen in this view, and its main buildings, a long stone block with a supplementary pedimented entrance, were on the north side.

Table 150

STOCKPORT, MANCHESTER (Central), WARRINGTON, WIDNES, and LIVERPOOL.

Week Days

A timetable for the CLC line between Manchester and Liverpool.

A BR Standard class 4 4–6–0 outside Trafford Park locoshed on 28 February 1965. In the background is an ex-LMS 2–6–4 tank loco. Trafford Park provided motive power for trains operating out of Manchester Central station, and over CLC metals. Trafford Park also had a subshed at Glazebrook. The joint ownership of the CLC was illustrated by the allocation of locos at the shed in January 1954, as both ex-LMS and ex-LNER locos were present. The BR Standard classes appeared from the late 1950s, as older ex-LNER types were withdrawn.

BR code 9E
Ex-LMS locos
Fowler 2–6–2T: 40009, 40017
Compound 4P 4–4–0: 40910, 41066, 41098, 41112, 41154, 41161, 41170, 41173
Fairburn 2–6–4T: 42064, 42065, 42676, 42683
Stanier 2–6–4T: 42452, 42469
4F 0–6–0: 44236, 44275, 44350, 44392
'Black Five' 4–6–0: 44717, 44938, 45239, 45347
'Jubilee' class 4–6–0: 45618 *New Hebrides*, 45622 *Nyasaland*, 45628 *Somaliland*, 45629 *Straits Settlements*, 45652 *Hawke*, 45655 *Keith*
8F 2–8–0: 48411, 48680, 48698, 48741
Ex-LNER locos:
Ex-GC D10 'Director' 4–4–0: 62653 *Sir Edward Fraser*, 62658 *Prince George*
Ex-GC D11 4–4–0: 62661 *Gerald Powys Dewhurst*, 62662 *Prince of Wales*, 62664 *Princess Mary*, 62668 *Jutland*
Ex-GC J10 0–6–0: 65138, 65144, 65146, 65153, 65156, 65157, 65167, 65170, 65171, 65181, 65184, 65186, 65187, 65191, 65197, 65198, 65205, 65209
Ex-GER J67 0–6–0T: 68583, 68595, 68598
Ex-GC N5 0–6–2T: 69255, 69304, 69326, 69335, 69336, 69343, 69347, 69358, 69361, 69364, 69370
Total: 72

The North Staffordshire Railway

The NSR had only one line into Cheshire, from Stoke-on-Trent to Manchester. Its most important station in the county was at Macclesfield, which is now electrified as part of the Manchester–Euston via Stoke-on-Trent route, now much busier than it was in steam days, due to weight limits at Harecastle Tunnel. In steam days, trains from Euston to Manchester usually ran via Crewe, as the NSR line via Stoke could not take the large LMS Pacific locos because of Harecastle Tunnel, and only secondary services used the line. Since electrification, however, most Manchester trains now run via Stoke and Macclesfield.

The NSR operated trains between Stoke and Macclesfield from October 1849, as a development of its line from Colwich to Macclesfield. Its station at Congleton is seen here at the turn of the century.

A Sentinel steam railcar at the NSR's Cheadle station, on the Cheshire–Staffordshire border.

Macclesfield station, which was rebuilt following electrification of the old NSR line between Colwich and Manchester Piccadilly. This was the furthest north reached by the NSR, which operated into Manchester courtesy of running powers over LNWR metals. A line between Colwich (on the Trent Valley line between Stafford and Rugby) and Macclesfield was authorized on 26 June 1846, and gave the Stoke company an alternative route from Manchester to London, away from the WCML of the LNWR, although friendly relations always existed between the two companies, despite the efforts of the LNWR to take control of the NSR. The line is still in use, having been electrified in the 1960s, and most Euston–Manchester trains use part of the line via Stoke-on-Trent, instead of operating through Crewe.

The modern signal-box at the old NSR Macclesfield station. The view was taken shortly after electrification, as the 1950s BR London Midland Region station nameboard is still there.

Acknowledgements

I would like to record my grateful thanks to everyone who has assisted with photographs and information for this project, including Peter Owen, Terry Roberts, Jim Roberts, Roger Carpenter, David Ibbotson, Mr A.G. Ellis and Lens of Sutton. Without their valued help, this project would have been so much more difficult to complete.